MARKET MIND GAMES

MARKET MIND GAMES

A Radical Psychology of Investing, Trading, and Risk

DENISE K. SHULL, M.A.

Mc
Graw
Hill
Education

New York   Chicago   San Francisco   Athens
London   Madrid   Mexico City   Milan
New Delhi   Singapore   Sydney   Toronto

1 2 3 4 5 6 7 8 9 10   DOC/DOC   1 6 5 4 3 2 1

ISBN   978-0-07-175622-8
MHID   0-07-175622-1

e-ISBN   978-0-07-176152-9
e-MHID   0-07-176152-7

McGraw-Hill Education books are available at special quantity discounts to use as premiums and sales promotions or for use in corporate training programs. To contact a representative, please visit the Contact Us pages at www.mhprofessional.com.

This book is printed on acid-free paper.

To my father, Wayne E. Shull, originally of Dover, Ohio, who first explained the stock market to me when I was nine. I said, "Really, you *own* parts of companies?" Little did I know then that he was the quintessential buy-and-hold investor. He began buying "T" (ATT) in the '40s and left it for me to sell. I am quite sure, because he said so, that he didn't know how to sell a share of stock. My becoming a trader, in 1994, met with what can only be called bemusement on his part.

Contents

Prologue
The Market's Masquerade

What if the mystery of market crashes and trader or investor meltdowns stems from a simple but total misunderstanding of our own minds? Could everything we think we know about ourselves—intelligence and rationality versus emotion and irrationality—be missing the mark?

Simply put—yes.

Connecting the dots across the vast fields in neuroscience shows that we actually perceive, judge, and decide in ways that operate almost in diametric opposition to the reigning theories in psychology and economics. Somewhere between Socrates and the mid-20th century rise of the cognitive behavioral school of psychology, we promoted intellect to chairman of the board. In reality, the wide-ranging category of feelings, which includes both conscious and unconscious emotion, owns all the shares.

Now I am by far not the first to say that we misunderstand how we really think.

Nassim Taleb told us in his runaway bestseller, *The Black Swan*, that "it looks like we have the wrong user's manual" and I could not agree more! The manual we need begins not with the assumed superiority of thought and reason but with the foundation of feeling and emotion, which contributes the meanings of anything and everything. For many decades now our attention has been focused almost exclusively on our thinking and our behavior. The more mysterious realm of feelings resided in the most relegated seat of all, that of being old, useless, and destructive. Ironically, linking together our failures to solve the mystery of meltdowns with the rapidly growing insights into how perceptions are formed proves that this dismissed realm belong front and center, first and foremost.

This overemphasis on our thinking (or cognition to use the academic term) underlies the second complaint of Taleb's, which I also agree with: the great intellectual fraud, or GIF, of the bell curve. This bedrock of the field of probability (and by extension the endeavor of market predictions) stems from the misplaced emphasis on the seemingly unique human ability to discover and apply the numerical disciplines of algebra, calculus, and theoretical mathematics. In fact, one can argue that a zealous belief in an ostensibly omnipotent power of numbers has misled us into our current reckoning with billion-dollar bonfires.

I do, however, part ways with Taleb when he says, "A small number of Black Swans explain almost everything in our world." If we take the whole of what we now know about how we perceive anything imprecise or conflicting (like market data), it won't be Black Swans that will do the explaining. It will be a totally new operating guide for a fully interactive psyche—fully reciprocal thinking, feeling, and emoting—that transforms his first identifier of "Black Swans"—"an outlier, as it lies outside the realm of regular expectations, because nothing in the past can convincingly point to its possibility"—into nicely bleached birds. Not only will many things that might escape expectation be expected, but they will easily fall into his lower standard of "the possible."

Taleb would almost certainly say that I am proving his third assertion—"in spite of outlier status, human nature makes us concoct explanations for its occurrence after the fact, making it explainable and predictable." But I am not talking about explaining after the fact, although better explanations of events do lead to an increase in knowledge overall; I am talking about the missing link in predicting. I am talking about picking up where our agreed upon GIF leaves off.

In plain English, I am simply saying that if we come to understand how we truly perceive, think, and decide—how all human brains take in, process, and act on data—that neither the explanations of randomness nor Black Swans will be so frequently needed. In fact, if we focus on the first one—perception—we will gain much. If we begin to incorporate the new realities of the sources of our own behavior in the market or in any high-risk decision, we will much more easily understand why we so often do that which we wish we wouldn't have.

The Provenance of This Book

Clearly, after centuries of debate in perception psychology, I am not writing just to be a writer. I intend to submit ideas that offer a theory that beats a theory—the unquestioned superiority of the intellect over the human realities of feeling and emotion. As such, I think it only fair that I explain how we got here.

In 2003, after updating for publication my master's thesis on unconscious patterns of perception and behavior and after nine years as a trader in a number of different environments, I had an idea about how understanding of conscious and unconscious emotions applied to trading. Gail Osten, now of the Chicago Board Options Exchange, found it interesting enough to publish the beginnings of the idea in the magazine, *SFO, Stock, Futures and Options*, which she then edited. Somewhat to my amazement, a handful of traders and portfolio managers called to ask for help in applying the ideas.

A few years later, my own futures broker asked me to speak publicly on my thoughts about emotions and market decisions. Now almost seven years later, I have had the unexpected, enlightening and frankly, delightful experience to teach my theory and its application to a few thousand people who daily deal in markets. A truly unexpected number of them have said, "That's it—you're right. This finally makes sense." One trader who attended a CME Group talk I gave for floor traders always says that he knew I was truly onto something when he watched 150 floor traders remain motionless in their seats for over an hour while I explained how one's unconscious needs and expectations could change a market decision. In 25 years of trading he had never seen floor traders sit still for anything! From his seat near the door he marveled that only one person left the room.

Finally, what even Taleb might agree with is that a highly unlikely number of these traders have reported notably more success with what turns out to be their relationship with—and not their probability analyses of—markets, risk, and uncertainty.

Market Mind Games outlines my attempt to curate all that I have learned in trading, investing, neuroscience, and consulting into one coherent, logical, and usable structure.

Here's the big picture of where we are going:

- Perception
- Beliefs as the foundation of judgment
- Judgment as the key to uncertainty
- The mind's recipe for making sense of "risk"
- The imperative of using emotions as data
- The natural law of contexts
- *fC* or feeling context—a physical state
- *eC* or emotional context—a type of *fC*
- The gargantuan role of the *F-eC* (or the fractal-emotional context)
- Managing to psychological and emotional capital
- Creating and re-creating psychological leverage

It doesn't matter if you look at this from the perspective of the group or the individual, whether you want to know how to make better portfolio and trading decisions for yourself, or whether you are at the Securities and Exchange Commission or Federal Reserve and you want to understand the minds and behaviors of professional traders. Billion dollar bonfires and market minion meltdowns stem from single matches of the mind being lit with the kindling of uncertainty.

Whether you care about the quickening pace of statistically improbable events or you simply want to play this market game at a higher level—not being beat by this *perceptual game* demands that you take on a gut-renovation of how you think about markets, unknowability, and bets on other people's future behavior.

Rethink the:

- Internal mind game or your own mental capital
- External mind games or the waves of perception that wash from one market-involved mind to the next—even if that mind uses a computer as translator

Again, like Taleb, this is not about behavior—it's about *thinking*.

Thinking about thinking is known as metacognition; and while the "how" of what to do is what everyone always wants to know, you need to thoroughly understand the *why* first. If you don't, you won't believe in it; and if you don't believe it, you can't feel it; and if you can't feel it, you won't—and actually cannot—do it. Oh, it might look like you do—for some time period equivalent to the average success on a diet, say—but soon, you will be in search of a new answer, strategy, or miracle.

"They" taught us—and we like to believe—that with our much larger frontal cortexes, the pinnacle of human intelligence lies in our skills of logic, reason, and math. While certainly clever, these abilities that have allowed mankind to deduce the underlying calculus and fractal geometry of nature, in fact, still depend completely on the senses, feelings, and emotions that came before.

Thinking relies on a fuel we have undervalued—our feelings, conscious and unconscious. First of all to do it, we need to want to understand something. That wanting? It is a feeling.

But that barely scratches the surface. Feelings include both sensory experiences—touch, tired, sore, for example (the bodily based sensations)—and emotional feelings, which we also feel in our bodies but in a different way than we feel tired or sick to our stomachs. The re-emergence, at least in Western culture, of the infinite loop of the body-brain-mind reveals the answers to the individual or societal frustrations of "Why do I do what I do?" or "How could they do what they do?" In other words, we feel feelings and emotions in our bodies and therefore we must include the "physical" in the mental.

The new imperative for deciphering and disentangling the mind games of markets, and of all uncertainty, lies in the individual experience of what I call the *fC*. This *fC* refers to the feelings context or context of feelings we bring to each and every perception we have, judgment we make, and decision we act on. It also follows then that looking at markets from the perspective of the collective *fCs* offers the student something much more useful than attempting to find the missing natural mathematical law.

Let me give you just a simple related example. In December 2010, the work of a special, presidentially appointed task force, the Financial Crisis Inquiry Commission, reportedly broke down. With a new context of confidence after the Republican rout of the November 2010 elections, a subgroup decided to release their own report and voted to ban from any final written report the words "Wall Street" and "shadow banking." Now of course, we just call this partisanship or a political circus. None of us were waiting with bated breath for the report anyway. But ask yourself: What is behind partisanship and political circuses? Isn't it always that one side holds one set of beliefs and the other side the opposite or at least highly dissimilar points of view?

Now think for a moment about what a belief or point of view even is. Wouldn't you say at a minimum that to have a point of view you have to believe in something? And to believe in something you have to have the confidence (this is one of those feeling things) that your belief is correct? This belief and its attendant feeling of confidence in its "rightness" is a context of feelings; in this case, the most important context—the *eC* or emotional context. Try as you might you will never truly be able to find an opinion, an analysis, or a decision that lacks an *eC*. Never. If that is not a natural law, I don't know what is!

Alas, You Need a New Spider Web

Given the prevailing opinion of feelings and emotions, this thesis might startle you. I mean, we like feelings and emotions in love, sports, and any kind of performance. Yet in decisions about risk; we categorically reject their value and usually blame any regrettable decision on the very existence of emotion.

Yet the hard cold truth is *an emotion alone never made or lost a dime.* That is a fact.

Only the actions that arise from or act out a feeling can make or lose money. Yet, for decades, we've put all our energy into thinking about thinking and behavior while disdaining and ignoring emotion. Blame the Greek philosophers or organized religion or your parents or whomever, but I am asking you to take a leap and benefit from eradicating all these ineffective assumptions that remain so widely reiterated.

Hence, I do need to provide a safety net, or at least some sturdy scaffolding. Think about learning something that you originally considered difficult but eventually "got." First, you "sort of" understood it. You might have been able to hear it and follow but you couldn't turn around and recount it. If you hear it again, however, a little more comes together. Your brain held in place some of the elements but it needed time to sort and organize and to connect new concepts into old knowledge. It repeats that process until you have new knowledge or skill. But it *always* needs a holding area.

Therefore, with a thesis built exclusively on the imperative but elusive and normally discarded arena of feelings, senses, emotions, and the unconscious, it will definitely help to have an at-the-ready staging area. If emotions in particular have long since been buried in a place you can't find, it will be very difficult—almost impossible—to internalize what is being said, even if you try. Not only will you not be able to recall or translate the information to share it with someone, you won't be able to begin to turn it into psychological leverage.

I also want to incorporate a fair amount of science. Luckily, it so happens that research shows we can understand logical questions better when they are put in human terms. I therefore owe you a new "spider web" or a mental staging area to at least catch the ideas and information while you put it together for yourself.

A Story of Market Mind Games

One craft of writing—storytelling—combined with our innate ability to more easily process information when it arrives in social or human terms elegantly solves the problem at hand. In other words, I've drafted a few *fictional* characters to help out. In the pages that follow, you will be joining them as they attend fictional versions of my typical lectures, workshops and consulting programs. Hopefully, their learning curve will shorten yours. More importantly, I hope they provide the practical bridge for what will be your own mental coup d'état over the mind games inherent in all markets. Let me introduce you to:

- Michael Kelley, an academic about to get a real shot at running money
- Richard Kelley, Michael's austere and judgmental father, who, like all parents, looms large in his conscious and unconscious mind
- Renee Smith, the daughter of a former floor trader
- Christopher Smith, Renee's father

As you and these figments of my imagination will see, the most enduring edge can be found within our own psyches.

Many clients tell me this approach changes not only their trading but their lives. Markets, and especially dealing with them, are microcosms of life. They simply masquerade as numerical puzzles.

Humans make markets and the human mind plays games—both on other human minds and on itself. Let's now recast the playing field in a way that brings you all the winning moves.

DKS, October 15, 2011

PART 1

PERCEPTION OR REALITY: WHAT MAKES MARKETS TICK?

Chapter 1

From Wall Street to the Ivory Tower and Back

Monday, April 18, 2011, 12:45 AM

Michael rolled his over stuffed duffle bag into the taxi queue at O'Hare. He'd stayed an extra day because the champagne powder just kept on coming but that meant he had just barely made it down the mountain in time to slip through the closing doors on the evening's last flight out of Denver. The 80 people now ahead of him combined with the 15 degree wind-chill compelled an audible, "You've got to be kidding!" Getting to ski with his younger brother Tom, while always a blast, drove a hard logistical bargain—particularly when he thought of the econ undergraduates he would be facing on maybe five hours of sleep.

"Oh well," he thought, "next year when I'm back to being the runt on the trading desk, I won't be skipping town for four days just because a blizzard rolls into Aspen."

A decade ago, Michael had been recruited to be a proprietary trader at Schoenberg Trading. He'd accepted against his father's will because in the late 1990s, the market seemed to print money—at least for anyone who understood the momentum game of stocks and because the day-to-day work actually felt to him a lot like chess, something he had excelled at even as a kid. For a few years, it was great. He could wear jeans, the firm bought lunch, and he was only supposed to trade from 8:30 to 11 and 1:30 to 3. The firm provided what were then cutting-edge analytics on the relative strength of each industry group and taught everyone to trade by buying the strong and selling the weak. It worked until it didn't.

Most of the guys learned how to be long stocks but when the Internet bubble burst, they couldn't, for some inexplicable reason, apply the same idea on the downside. The firm closed their Chicago office and in the fall of the 2002 bear market, Michael returned to Chicago University for his MBA. He thought taking on a purely quantitative view of markets would be the best alternative.

After he got to Chicago, however, he found the classes too management focused. He cared about markets. Of course, Chicago as an institution had a long history of market theory; so with a little finagling, he segued out of financial analysis and into decision theory—a PhD track. For a while it felt exhilarating just to be able to cogitate. He had grown up immersed in books and spending his days contemplating models of decision making suited him just fine.

In the aftermath of 2008, however, headhunters surprisingly began to call. He wasn't even sure how they found him. He wasn't big on LinkedIn, Twitter, or Facebook and didn't have anything resembling a raging social life. He turned the first two down flat. He had no interest in pumping out a bunch of data that some portfolio manager or marketing type would use for raising capital but otherwise cast aside. Eventually, however, when the offer clearly included the chance to sit on the trading desk and potentially manage a portfolio himself, he could no longer resist. Inside, he realized he really did want very much to return to *"running money."*

Michael's father, Richard, predictably had criticized Michael's decision. He had loaned Michael part of the $100,000 tuition and would tolerate slow payback as long as Michael stuck with academia. He didn't approve the first time Michael had gone to Wall Street, and his return lit up something akin to a simmering rage. Richard Kelley believed that speculators abjectly lacked morals and, even though he dealt with hedge funds in his role as chief financial officer at an insurance company, he pejoratively referred to them as "necessary evils."

Finally, through his haze of half-awake thoughts, Michael realized that the people behind him were inching in on him. A bevy of cabs arrived and the line lurched forward—putting him face-to-face with a tall brunette he'd noticed on campus once or twice. Instantaneously weighing the benefits of jumping the line versus humiliation, he summoned his most gentlemanly voice and asked, "Pardon me, but don't I see you around at Chicago U?" It worked.

In the cab, Renee explained her graduate work in the university's Biopsychology Institute. At first, Michael admitted he needed the layman translation of "researching the reciprocity between mind and body all the way down to cellular mechanisms and their ties to behavior and social context." Renee gave it another try not yet knowing herself Michael's reason for being at Chicago U. "Well, look," she said, "for a long time and even today in some circles, not only is the mind different than the brain but the brain is virtually detached from the body—at least in terms of theories about how we think and decide. The work in my department brings all three back together."

Michael, as a decision researcher himself felt intrigued. "Amazing" he said. "I teach undergrads out of the decision research center over on Hyde Street."

"Really? I didn't know we had a Decision Center."

"Well, right back at you" he said with a smile. "I've been here for over eight years and never heard of a Biopsychology Institute!"

"Guess we're even then," she said with a laugh. "So what exactly does this decision department do, anyway?"

"Well, if you read the brochures, they say we study 'the processes by which intuition, reasoning, and social interaction produce beliefs, judgments, and choices.' Most people think we are the behavioral economics department but labeling it as 'behavior' narrows the scope to what seems to me to be just the end result. I mean, what causes the behavior?"

"Exactly," said Renee. "Basically, that's our philosophy too!"

Abruptly, he realized they'd arrived on campus. Michael insisted Renee be dropped off first, and he wouldn't let her give him more than $15 for the $42 fare. "I got to jump the line to ride with you, so we're square," he said. As he stuffed the bill in his pocket, he happily realized her card was sandwiched within the money.

Monday Afternoon, April 18, 2011

With a noontime nap under his belt and a Quad Grande Latte at his side, Michael settled into reading the stack of opinion essays he'd received that morning. The first one was entitled, "Markowitz & Beliefs."

Harry Markowitz had won a Nobel Prize for figuring out what back in 1952 was called "Modern Portfolio Theory" and for what some consider the first truly quantitative approach to asset allocation. This title suggested the student had a psychological take on the mathematical approach. "Hmmm ... interesting," thought Michael just as he heard his father's ring tone. Seemingly always at the worst moment, Richard called. He probably only wanted to find out what his brother Tom was up to. When they were kids, Dad always favored Tom, the jock. Michael's GPA never garnered much enthusiasm (or even attention for that matter); but after Tom got cut from the US ski team and moved to Aspen to patrol, his father rarely, if ever, spoke to him. He used Michael—or tried to use him— as his messenger. Michael hit IGNORE and assuaged his guilt by telling himself he would call him back when he'd finished grading this stack of papers.

Somehow three hours then evaporated and Michael wanted a break. The sun shone through his windows and the temperature outside seemed to have sky-rocketed. As he rounded the first corner on his way back to Starbucks, he stopped into the department office to see if anyone wanted to join him.

"Michael, good to see you! I was just wondering when you were coming back," said Professor Zannis, Michael's dissertation advisor and one of the bedrocks in the department.

"Say," he continued, "A few weeks ago, I agreed to jointly sponsor a guest lecture series with a professor in the psychology department and I thought, given that it has a Wall Street bent, it would be right up your alley."

"Really? … what's the actual subject?" said Michael.

"Well, you probably haven't heard of them but we have a department here called the Biopsychology Institute, and a long-time friend of mine over there recommended we invite one of their graduates who runs a consulting firm on Wall Street—a woman named Denise Shull—to speak on what she calls the new psychology of risk, uncertainty, and decision making. It sounded like a provocative topic for the Spring Friday series, so I went with it."

"That's mildly amazing actually. I just met a woman from that department last night in the cab line. I didn't know they existed! When is it?"

"Well that's the thing, in only a few weeks, so I was hoping you would help get the word out. There is draft flyer on the printer now. Let me know what you think. You've been around here long enough to know what might entice our quirky but lovable geeks to show up for a talk on something other than esoteric models."

"Aha," Michael laughed. "Maybe the angle of a room full of female psychology grads might get some traction." After all, having met Renee, the pitch already worked for him.

Chapter 2

Numbers Look You in the Eye and Lie

Day 1: Special Lecture: A (Radical) New Psychology of Risk
Chicago University

May 13, 2011

"So without further ado, I would like to introduce our speaker, Denise Shull," said Michael, as he took a seat beside Renee.

Thank you, Michael, and thank you, everyone, for being here. Let's jump right in.

2 plus 2 equals 4. There are no if, ands, or buts about it. Express it in Chinese and 2 plus 2 does not magically morph into 6, despite the beauty of the characters or the evidence that different cultures learn math in different parts of the brain.

2 and 4 in a different context, however, can mean any number of things. Deceptively, 2 times 2 still equals 4. 2 minus 2, however, equals zero. Go to point two (.2) and you could mean 2/10ths or

1/5th of a whole—as in the answer you give Grandma when she asks how much of her scrumptious gooey pecan pie you want her to cut (you've got four relatives at the table); or, you could mean you have a 20% chance of losing all of the money you risked on a poker hand, a real estate investment, a decision for a new business, or a simple options trade wherein you bought calls on the off-chance AAPL might dip below $320.

Clearly, even in simple arithmetic, the purest of numerical disciplines, any given number only means something in the context of what sits next to it—plus, minus, times.

If a percentage sign sits next to it, well, honestly, despite the reliance on probabilities for betting, *all bets are off*. When we enumerate chance, we enumerate uncertainty. Unfortunately, the satisfaction we experience from enumeration tricks us into thinking we have waved the magic wand and remodeled 20% into 2 plus 2 equals 4.

Numbers make us feel good. We know we appear erudite, and we privately feel exceptionally smart if we find or have a set of numbers that argues for our point of view. We tend to feel particularly self-satisfied if we possess a set of numbers that appears to prove something that we are the first to figure out.

But have you said or ever heard someone say, "Just because I can"?

It's an idiom and an attitude typically chuckled about behind closed doors, but I'd wager that most of us in this room have either said it ourselves or been tempted to applaud when our best buddy uttered it.

However, isn't the subtext of such a statement, "Well, maybe I should have but probably I shouldn't have but I did it anyway just because I could," or, "I felt like it, wanted to, or thought no one would know"?

Expectations

And there we have the crux of many matters of human decision making and behavior—perceived consequences or the lack thereof.

We do what we do because we expect the things we *want* to occur as the result. Likewise, we also don't do what we don't do because we expect that if we did, things would happen that we expect would be, "umm, well ... unpleasant."

Expectations about the future, particularly how we imagine we will feel, serve as the cornerstone for deciding whether or not we drink that third glass of wine, run that mile, or say something provocative to our boss. Now, in each of these work-a-day world cases, we can come very close to a precise prediction about what will happen—we will wake up with a headache, we will feel more energized, or we will suffer grating wrath.

Yet, what do we do when we can't be so sure of the consequences? How do we choose our actions when the information available in the present fails to be enough to know what to expect? (Like say when it comes to predicting whether the value of a stock, bond, or commodity will go up.)

The Seduction of Statistics

Particularly when it comes to markets, we turn to the mechanisms of statistics and probability—those certain kinds of numbers that make us feel we have measured the future, but in reality only deceive us into thinking we know what we need to do. ***Reality points to a very big gap between where the numbers leave off and exceptional performance begins!*** Traditional trading education repeatedly advises students to "analyze what confluence of circumstances you are looking for, know what outcomes they have led to in the past and when they re-occur, take the trade." Likewise, if you don't see the same situation, do nothing.

Peter Bernstein wrote in his market classic, *Against the Gods: The Remarkable Story of Risk,* that mankind's modern times began when we learned to understand, measure, and weigh the consequences of risk. Normally (if there is such a thing), markets—bonds, stocks, commodities—don't all trade in the same direction at the same time. Stocks go up while bonds go down. Markets that appear to not trade with any relationship to one another—something like AAPL and Spanish government debt might be marked at .1. Take the stocks of big USA-based technology companies and it wouldn't be uncommon to find correlations marked at .7 or .8. Offsetting risk in one market simply required being active in another, relatively uncorrelated one.

The MBAs here of course understand this; the psychology gang, I realize that you may or may not.

Yet, no less than the CEO of Goldman Sachs himself called the violent market swings of August 2007 a 25th deviation event. According to the discipline of probability, what we saw with our own eyes could not happen—not in our lifetimes or the lifetimes of all of our ancestors and all of our children, grandchildren, and their great grandchildren. Then a mere 13 months later, markets stunned the entire planet when every single one went simultaneously in one direction—another thing that, statistically speaking, could not happen.

Theoretically, given our 21st-century capacity to capture every minute detail of a pattern (and to react to it within milliseconds), the earlier excruciatingly painful whipsaws of 1929 or 1987 wouldn't re-occur. Yet, in the 21st century, in each successively larger billion-dollar bonfire, from 1997 to 2001 to 2008, the world elite of Bernstein's measurers had indeed measured not only once, not only twice, but a hundred times.

Today in the spring of 2011, the gut-wrenching days of 2008 may be fading from our memories, but one thing is for sure. Despite widespread blame of alleged greedy bankers, it makes no sense to believe that they expected to lose money. It makes no sense that dedicated life-long employees who invested all of their retirement accounts in the stocks of their own companies, BSC and LEH in particular, expected, probabilistically or otherwise, for their companies, monies, and lives to go up in the smoke of billion-dollar bonfires. Indictments of greed are overrated as useful explanations or contributions to solutions.

In fact, many were looking at numbers that had been analyzed every which way from Sunday and that still showed money coming in the door—practically right up until the moment that it stopped. A few outsiders "interpreted" the numbers a different way and made literally billions of dollars. Reportedly, Matthew Tannin of Bear Stearns had a sense—not a number—that caused him to alert his boss to the possibility that the numbers weren't telling the whole truth—numbers that landed them both in court.

Nevertheless, PhDs in fields like physics, game theory, and theoretical math at esteemed firms like Renaissance spend every day dreaming up new ways to slice and dice the latest probabilities hidden in whatever the current mood of the markets seems to be. But you've got to wonder: if it truly was a matter of uncovering the market data equivalent of $E=mc^2$, then wouldn't they have found it by now? Or, doesn't the fact that they keep looking, in and of itself, prove that at best any probabilistic viewpoint is only temporarily relevant? And if only temporarily relevant, how do they detect when the relevance ends?

Logically, if you have a probability that you know will apply for only a limited period of time and by definition that probability tells you that you have some significant chance of being wrong, even while it still applies, how much do you really know?

So, my question to you is: "Just because we can, does it mean we should?" Or, even more to the point, just because we can dazzle one another with complex mathematical feats, does it mean we have been more "rational" because we have been numerical?

Our Distaste for Imprecision

With the few exceptions like Nassim Taleb and his Black Swans or Benoit Mandelbrot, almost everyone who purports to be an expert on predicting markets preaches the probability gospel.

Mandelbrot discovered fractal geometry and showed convincingly in his books, *The (mis)Behavior of Markets* and *Fractals and Scaling in Finance*, that the uneven reality of markets matches up much better with patterns that you find in cauliflower or broccoli than with bell curves.

But given the relative paucity of applications of his work, it would appear his ideas ran into the resistance of what, time and time again, academic experimenting has demonstrated—that we *greatly* prefer to know what exactly our odds are. We feel more confident and less anxious when we know or *think we know* our exact chances. Known as the "ambiguity aversion," many decision theorists have shown that game players greatly prefer to play a game where they choose between 50 red and 50 black balls versus a game where they have 100 balls but don't know the exact mix of colors. Daniel Ellsberg demonstrated it, but many others, including John Maynard Keynes, are reported to have declared the same result.

Renee, somewhat to Michael's surprise, raised her hand. "Ms. Shull, aren't you saying that managing money ends up being a lot like playing poker? You have got the cards and their odds, but that isn't really the game?"

Yes indeed, Renee, poker offers a great example of what I'm talking about. (Or maybe I should say winning at poker does!) For instance, listen to inexperienced poker players talk about the game. They will wax on about it being only about the odds of the cards. No matter what you say, they will just talk about the numbers. But ask the traders I know who also are skilled poker players and every one of them will tell you that winning is NOT about the stats. The novices want to believe that, but if you watch high-stakes poker, where by definition the players have a proven ability to win, you often see sunglasses and baseball caps. What does obscuring your vision have to do with a purely numbers game? Stories abound of another oddity in poker—playing without ever looking at one's cards! If it is only about the numbers, how could anyone *ever* do that?

Indeed, poker provides numerous market decision parallels.

An Irrefutable Fact—Even If We Don't Like It

It is impossible to know the future.

After all, being the future, it has not happened yet.

"Live in the moment" may be the mantra of many a hedonist and Eastern philosopher alike, but in the ever-quickening pace of a world on a non-stop grid, most lives roll from one decision about the future to the next. In the moment or in the macro, starting about the time our parents let us stay home alone for the first time, we begin very clearly deciding what is and what isn't worth it and what will be the likely outcome of a choice. Yes, we get a little lackadaisical about it during the hormone rush of high school — even so, whether we should or shouldn't play soccer, join the drama club, date that wild-child guy, try to get into Harvard, sleep through Art History 101 simply because we can — it all boils down to what we perceive and therefore believe the future will bring if we choose A, B, or C. Our imaginations paint a picture of what life will feel like if we do this or if we do that.

As time passes, what we imagine may turn out that "there is nothing new under the sun," and then again, it might not. In fact there may indeed be a better than 51% probability that the future will look like the past, but what about the other 49%? Unless time travel becomes a reality, we have literally *no* way of knowing the "anythings" that can happen in the next moment, month, or month after that.

Things that have never happened before happen *all the time*. In this day and age of nanosecond global communication, at a very minimum, everything happens faster and more people know about it instantaneously. This means that reactions occur more quickly and just the dimension of speed creates phenomena never seen before. To a great degree, that technological change *alone* added fuel to the trillion dollar travesties of the recent past.

Data crunching had indeed lured bankers to get more creative. Lots of money was floating around and it seemed to need to go somewhere. So almost all of a sudden, it became a good idea to lend money with no documentation and to give mortgages to people without bothering about down payments. The numbers they used to predict what would happen indicated that while, yes, there would be defaults, the number or character of those defaults wouldn't create a problem. The amount of number crunching fueling these creative statistical analyses probably surpassed the totality of mortgage number crunching for the previous 50 years.

But alas, as we all know all too well—the numbers lied.

The same applies to life's unspeakable tragedies and everyday annoyances. On Monday evening September 10, 2001, in New York, the suffocating humidity of afternoon thunderstorms or Donald Rumsfeld on TV talking about the military budget gave no clue about the terrorist warfare about to ensue.

In the less catastrophic mundane circumstances of most days, we break our fingers, dent our cars, and even catch colds—all when we aren't expecting it. We thought we were on our way to soccer, going to win the game, and then study for the GMAT. Instead, we are at the body shop alone with a splint on our finger and pain pills in our pocket, while our buddies brood about their loss over a beer.

Of course, insurance companies have a rather detailed idea of how many broken fingers, dented fenders, and cases of the flu will occur over a large group of people. Ask an insurance executive, however, who exactly is going to dent their car and their rep will conclude that he or she should add mental health risk to your profile!

In March 2011, an earthquake led to a tsunami that led to a partial nuclear and market meltdown in Japan. Systematic or purely numbers-based systems got whipsawed into a money-losing month. Taleb categorizes such events in the lake of the Black Swans, but do we really have to live with that? Do we just have to expect that we can never know more and predict more accurately? I submit that we don't—if we are brave enough to look beyond the numbers.

The truth is: Probabilities tell us something—just not everything.

And as anyone who is a stickler about honesty will say, knowingly omitting crucial information, even without directly lying, amounts to telling a lie. Omissions can and do easily mislead.

Numbers Limitations: Neuron Limitations— A Coincidence?

Michael had to bristle a bit. What about all the successful computerized strategies running in the markets today? He himself had been approached to join a firm that wanted his help in reverse-engineering market data to deduce the probabilities of oncoming human perception in a variety of market scenarios.

But before he could raise his hand, it was almost like Ms. Shull read his mind and responded.

Believing in the penultimate power of numbers, some money managers market the idea that they have programmed neural networks into their market-stalking computers. Sure, it sounds sexy and sophisticated; but at a minimum, overstates reality and at a maximum, can't be true.

Despite Paul Allen's newly announced atlas of the brain, we would be hard pressed to find a neuroscientist on the planet who can tell you *precisely* how a neural network operates or, more importantly, what chemical, electrical, and other processes specifically give rise to thought. To the layperson, it sounds like we know this because we get news flash after news flash regarding this or that part of the brain being responsible for this or that. But in reality, that knowledge typically relies on associating areas of the brain with tasks through an fMRI machine and can't technically prove causation or even be regarded as a finely calibrated tool!

My point? If we don't actually know how something works, then how can we presume to duplicate it?

Even more importantly, however, recent research reveals the whole idea of a neural network as the model for the brain to be grossly incorrect. Known as the "neural doctrine" in academia, the idea actually is an artifact of early research, like the original geocentric idea of the solar system. Actually, neurons make up only about 15% of the brain. The rest has until very recently been relegated to the term "junk."

Indulge me in a bit of neuroscience here as I think it will help you be able to absorb the gravity of the need to rethink our dependence on numbers—and, in fact, rethink thinking altogether.

Neurons and synapses work with an electrical charge passed through a liquid chemical substrate; what in this day and age we all know as neurotransmitters. To date, all of our mental capacities have been assumed to emerge from this electro-chemical communication. The other classes of brain tissues known as glia cells were thought to simply clean up any extra fluid or voltage.

The Truth About Neurons

The key word there is "were." Now we know that the cells formerly assigned to janitor duty communicate "without" electricity, and in a model more like a broadcast than a node-to-node network. It gets even better, or at least even more revolutionary. These cells not only sense the electricity coursing through the neurons and synapses but have the power to change, modify, or even control it! R. Douglas Fields recently wrote in his book, *The Other Brain*, "Glia are the key to understanding this new view of the brain."

Work done on Einstein's brain helps prove his point. A careful counting of Einstein's neurons versus 11 other male brains showed essentially the same number of neurons in all 12. The difference, however, in Einstein's brain tissue showed up in the glia. The 11 comparative samples of brain tissue, from men in their middle to older ages, had one glia for every two neurons. In Einstein's brain the ratio was 1-to-1 or twice as many "neural glue" cells. According to Fields, the biggest differential in neurons to glia existed in areas known for abstract concepts and complex thinking. Glia clearly not only aren't junk but they may be the greater arbiter of a type of intelligence we all recognize.

In short, numbers in fact are relatively easy. They are clean and clear and, as we have agreed, make us feel secure. But time and time again, we have manipulated them and they have manipulated us into false senses of security. Maybe we just have to step up and admit we shouldn't trust them anywhere nearly as much as we do.

What Makes an Electrical Counting Machine Smart?

Maybe the other quant buzz word of 2011, "machine learning," holds the missing mathematical clue. After all, IBM's Watson beat two human *Jeopardy* champions, relying purely on the 0s and 1s that underlie all computing firepower. Isn't that proof enough that numbers alone in the end will still win? No, indeed it is not. First of all, there was a known answer to every question Watson answered. Watson had "read" all of Wikipedia and enormous amounts of historical and current texts. "He" had analyzed plays and movies. Yes, this anthropomorphized computer performed brilliantly, but every question already had a known answer.

More importantly, what tends to escape everyone's notice is how IBM's Watson emulated the actual human decision-making process. Can anyone think what I mean by that statement? I'll give you a clue. Watson calculated a number for it before he decided to answer.

Furthermore, the government releases a monthly numerically interpreted version of "IT" but as an entity, it proves to be elusive, ephemeral, and instantaneously changeable. In any team sport or for any athlete in general, it can reverse and reverse again within moments. The play goes well and the running back scores, and "it" appears. They run the kick back for a responding touchdown, and "it" disappears.

Yet Watson, an inorganic, electrically driven player depended on "it," or the simulation of "it," to win at *Jeopardy*. If his calculated confidence level, the "it", wasn't high enough, he didn't ring the *Jeopardy* bell. Is that machine learning, or are machines emulating humans?

I submit that if a computer figures out how confident it "feels" about something, then indeed the discovery says more about us than it does about our ability to give a computer enough information to deduce answers to known questions.

Excellence Doesn't Automatically Emerge From Numbers

The bottom line? We all know that we can get the numbers to say just about anything we want. What comes before, the context, and what we infer, or what comes after, from our models makes the difference in what we expect.

Wouldn't we therefore be able to extract a powerful advantage if we spent more time logically analyzing what the numbers *cannot* tell us?

Chapter 3

Mis-Remembering the
Caveats of the Early Quants

Day 2: Special Lecture on a New Psychology of Risk
Chicago University

May 20, 2011

Thanks, everyone, for returning for a second Friday afternoon! I want
to begin our second lecture with a real-life story from the summer
of 1994 and my days trading in Chicago.

I found myself out water skiing very early on an August morning
in Lake Geneva, the beautiful lake north of Chicago sometimes
known as the Newport of the Midwest. My good friend, Don, who
was known as "ZAP" on trading floors, owned the boat; but as it
turned out, it had at one time belonged to the third person who was
in the boat with us, a guy named Richard who at that time lived in
Santa Monica. Over piping hot coffee and right-off-the-griddle
donuts, I inquired why the boat was now Don's when it had once
been Richard's.

"To raise a new stake," they said with a tad of incredulity.

I didn't get it. Being at the time, the daughter of a buy-and-hold … and hold and hold … family, I had trouble imagining what they were saying and putting it together with a 17-foot inboard engine ski boat. As it turns out, Richard had, well, let's just say he had a very bad day back on 1987's Black Monday. He, as it was explained to me, broke the first rule of trading: *live to trade another day.*

It means, no matter what you do, no matter how appealing adding to a position or letting it trade further against you, everyone is supposed to know that you *never* ever risk everything.

But see, Richard was an options trader—arguably the most justifiably probabilistic of trading styles. And to make a long story short, he essentially forgot what we talked about last week; or, to put it another way, while the odds were way against the sell-off of 1987, that didn't make getting long on the Friday before a good idea! Or, again in short:

- Probabilities tell you something—but not everything.
- New scenarios occur all the time.

I understand that market players resist the reality that models can never be more than approximations. I know that the line between where the model ends and the judgment ensues varies. (But, hey, isn't that why we get paid the big bucks, by the way?) And, yes, I know about Fischer Black and Myron Scholes (and their competitors) who produced a very useful options pricing model that can come very close, at certain points, to predicting the exact prices.

Nevertheless, the key words there are "very close to" versus exact.

The delta between the two—very close and exact—looms large.

Risk Versus Uncertainty

It comes down to what one historical market master defined as the difference between risk and uncertainty. Most of us would think they are the same, but I think you will find it interesting that this question has been around for a long time and actually a clear and known difference in definition exists. In 1921, Frank Knight declared it in his classic book, *Risk, Uncertainty, and Profit*:

> *To preserve the distinction ... between the measurable uncertainty and an unmeasurable one we may use the term "risk" to designate the former and the term "uncertainty" for the latter.*

Ninety years and incalculable amounts of measuring power later does not change the fact that the only thing about the future that we can be sure of is the turning of the Earth and the attendant sunrises and sunsets. We know nothing else for sure other than time will march on.

In money running, however, let's say that your models indicate there will be a downturn in big cap tech stocks like GOOG and AAPL. Would it tell you exactly when that would begin and for how long it will last? Would it tell you the exact minute when it would reverse? Of course not. We all know that these things are impossible to predict; yet we forge full steam ahead with our ever more complex analyses, as if some piece of data will magically reveal the missing details.

Obviously, infinitely more data points *are* measurable today than in Knight's days. We can see inside the human skull and map the relative size of major parts of the brain. We can watch the blood flow from one area of the brain to another and when matched up with a given task (like playing cards or picking stocks), we can see how long it takes for a decision to be made about something that is certain versus something that is not. Nevertheless, just because we now have the technology to see where we couldn't and the instrumentation to measure a molecule doesn't automatically mean we have eradicated the reality of unmeasurability.

Dice or Poker Anyone?

Let's return to our poker analogy that we began last week and contrast it with another game of chance.

To Knight, risk means literally rolling dice. Poker, on the other hand, illustrates uncertainty. In a pure roll of the dice, *only* 11 outcomes can occur. Added together, the sum of the numbers on the two die can only result in a number between 2 and 12. The probabilities of getting a 2 versus a 4 versus or 6 differ from one another because there are multiple combinations that roll 4 or 6 (5 and 1 or 2 and 2 for a 4, let's say); whereas only 1 that adds up to 2, but nothing except die that have been tampered with will ever change the odds, probability, or chance of rolling a 2. Furthermore, while we don't need to do the calculation here, we could determine the exact chances of rolling any given number because there are a finite and immutable set of outcomes.

Conversely, while many people think of poker as a probability game, they err. Maybe they can fairly say half of the game consists of such numbers, but it wouldn't be hard to find hordes of good players who would disagree. Sure, only so many combinations of cards can be held or played; and while you need a computer to help you figure out all of the permutations in which cards can be dropped, what about when the fun begins?

When the wagering begins, uncertainty sets in!

Winners in poker rely on the human perception games of the betting. An effectively limitless number of outcomes are possible when human choice enters the picture.

Theoretically, I suppose a computer could even calculate all of the possible bets for all the possible combinations and sequences of cards; but even if you had that, you would never know, you could never know, if the bettor was bluffing. And then, even if you added a bluff/no-bluff (computers like those either/or questions) dimension to the mountain of data you had, what about the next hand? Or what if someone left the game and a new player came in? Could you ever accurately predict the betting patterns of every player who might sit at your table? Worse, what if they ordered one too many Scotches? Would their betting change?

We could go on but hopefully you get the point. The cards give you a framework—something to work with to anchor how you begin to think about the game.

If you want to win, however, you will need to assess the meaning, intention, and veracity of your opponents' plays. Yet those critical dimensions cannot be measured in anything that even vaguely represents precision. No one ever knows for sure what the player to his left will do or what someone on his right has in his hand! I don't know whether Frank Knight played poker or not. I do know that winning at it means you are dealing well with what today's game theorists recognize as Knightian uncertainty.

Call and Raise

Now, let's suppose you want to be a player in the global game of the markets. You've just been called and raised in the matter of uncertainty. At least in poker, you only have four suits and 52 cards to deal with. It doesn't take a track record in calculus to see that investing, managing money, or trading gives you orders of magnitude of more possibilities, and therefore more combinations, than a card game. How many stocks can you trade? In the United States? In Brazil? What about bonds? How many currencies? What about arbitrages or ETFs (exchange-traded funds)? And I mean, heaven forbid, you speculate in oil!

Add to that that neither the cards nor time runs out. Prices just keep on changing and either changing back or continuing in a direction. And some weeks those changes make the weather look like an exact science!

Think back to March 2008. Bear Stearns traded on $70 on Monday, $50 on Thursday, $30 on Friday, and $2 before the end of the weekend. In just seven days, the sentiment of climate change turned North Carolina into the North Pole!

Or take the party that was 1999 if you want to see the reverse. IPOs of companies with an inkling of an idea for the Internet began trading on the NYSE at 9:30 at a price set primarily by demand and oftentimes within moments—their prices floated upward like a balloon accidentally released into a strong wind over Lake Michigan. Today, we are starting to see some of this again. Take the IPO of the business networking site LinkedIn, which almost did the same thing.

We could go on and on and on with examples. In today's Twitter time, word travels fast, and any tradable asset can find itself in the grips of a run or a push in literally an instant. Regardless of the intended timeframe— 10 seconds, minutes, days, or years—the irrefutable unknowability of a stock's future price remains as unassailable as gravity.

Price Can Only Be Perception's Reflection

Price depends on perception.

As with poker, no inorganic matter offers much assistance in predicting with any accuracy the twists and turns of human opinion.

Yes, I know … facing this tends to induce an argument—either "but that is what probability is for" or the worry of "where does that leave us?"

Those protestations frankly prove our aversion to ambiguity.

I suggest, however, that you will fare better when you face reality, admit to the anxiety, and accept the game you want to play for what it is. English footballers may prefer there be timeouts as in American football. But what would happen to their teams if they played in denial of the reality that there are not? I think you would agree that it might be impossible to consistently play anything well if you approach it *without* an understanding of the true playing field.

"May I ask a question?" Michael asked as he half raised his hand. "On one hand, I totally see your point and I think it makes sense. On the other, however, I am wondering, given that the vast majority of market players have always treated the markets like a numbers and

probability game, couldn't you still say that, all in all, it hasn't been that bad? I mean, here we sit, back at Dow 12,000. The market seems to always bounce back from whatever 'dislocations,' as they call them, come around. Is it fair to say that no one can 'consistently play well'?"

That's a fair question, Michael. I think the focus, however, needs to be not on the fact that somehow, someway, we get market rebounds but more on the lack of widespread understanding of how major drops occur. They happen on a regular basis, yet, while a lot of words have been written, most of Wall Street will kind of shrug their shoulders and say that major swoons are either inevitable or are "simply" unknowable Black Swans.

Conversely, I think that the players who put all of the numbers and probabilities in their proper contexts can indeed truly consistently and reliably play well. In fact, our next topic reveals a very useful bit of irony to help.

The Irony of One of the First Real Quants

First we had "Uncertainty Frank" over at the University of Chicago, and then along came another insightful gentleman named Harry with his seminal 1952 paper, "Portfolio Selection," in the prestigious *Journal of Finance*. A newly minted PhD, Dr. Harry Markowitz revolutionized the conventional wisdom regarding investing.

Markowitz argued that if people actually enacted one of the popular recommendations of the time—choosing only stocks with the highest dividends—the logical end point lay in having one and only one stock in a portfolio. On the other hand, if portfolios had different mixes of assets, then the risk would be spread out across investments that typically behaved differently. Put 60% in stocks, 30% in bonds, and 10% in cash. Next, break down the percentages invested in stocks and bonds and even the cash into different "nationalities." Pick some higher volatility stocks and some lower, some plodding big caps, and some smaller companies. Risk factors could be assigned to each, and in the end you would have a wide range of "risk" levels that would at least theoretically, as Bernstein later declared, balance out the scales.

Sixty years later, it cannot be overstated how far-reaching Markowitz's concept of asset allocation became. The idea of spreading "risk" across asset classes and specific investments or trades within a given class causes CNBC to flash "headline news" when firms like Blackrock or Goldman Sachs change their recommended allocations. Financial advisors for all practical purposes exist to do one thing—help investors spread capital across markets and assets that should behave differently, trade in opposite directions, and never put anyone in the position of failing to live to trade another day. It would take a lot of searching to find someone knowledgeable about the markets who doesn't believe in spreading eggs across baskets. It's the conventional wisdom's bedrock of how to always live to trade another day.

There's just one problem—one of those "devil is in the details" situations that need to be either considered, if it ever was considered, which given our love affair with numbers is doubtful, or re-considered.

We Ignored Markowitz's Step One!

When Markowitz shared the Nobel Prize in 1990, he explained that while interested in philosophy initially, he subsequently became intrigued with "the economics of uncertainty." He admitted to always having given thought to applying mathematical techniques to problems of uncertainty and when it came "time to choose a topic for my dissertation; a chance conversation suggested the possibility of applying mathematical methods to the stock market."

I would like to know his thoughts on Knight, who we can imagine may have thought he shouldn't waste his time or talent on the immeasurable; but as it turns out, his application of math always existed in a context that absolutely gave nod to Knightian uncertainty.

It may come as a great surprise to many of you, but Markowitz's first paragraph states:

The process of selecting a portfolio may be divided into two stages. The first stage starts with observation and experience and ends with beliefs about the future performances of available securities. The second stage starts with the relevant beliefs about future performances and ends with the choice of a portfolio. This paper is concerned with the second stage.

What? This paper starts with the second stage? Did he really say that?

So what happened to the first? And how can the whole world of finance, investing, and trading have skipped step one? Honestly, I don't know how they did it. I don't know how market academicians and real-world Wall Streeters ignored this for six decades; but I can promise you, in our minds, in what makes our decisions, lay our all-important beliefs. Those beliefs architect and color what we see. Markowitz wanted us to keep that in the forefront of our minds. People want markets to be fully quantifiable. They want that certainty. Some are rumored to believe there is natural law–type truth somewhere in the patterns. But could skipping over the foundation—analyzing the beliefs that build the numbers—be the turn where we went (and still go) wrong? Markowitz himself couldn't really emphasize this point enough. Later in the paper he said it again: "This paper does not consider the difficult question of how investors do (or should) form their probability beliefs."

Before we go any further, let's take a stab at what he called "difficult." Let's say that in September 2008, you firmly believed in the widely held market view of "reversion to the mean." After all, September 2007 saw dizzying drops only to see all-time highs in October. Wouldn't that strengthen your belief in "what goes down, must come up"? So if you held that belief, what would have been the right thing to do when markets started dropping in absolute terms like never before or at least in a way you personally had never seen?

"Buy, buy, buy, Mortimer!" Right?

How would that have worked out?

While it may be a bit hard to untangle what we believe from what we analyze, we can see from afar how a particular mindset would underlie a particular set of decisions.

I think we can even go one step further and imagine how your basic market suppositions, reversions or trend following, would also influence whatever model one wanted to build.

There is an old saying in academia, "Torture the data long enough and it will confess."

You Need a Belief to Curate the World

We all like to believe we are objective. But in reality, we have to have beliefs to get through the day. If we didn't, we couldn't or wouldn't make simple choices, such as what is appropriate to wear, or how much wiggle room we have with the speed limit, or how important it is to do our best at a task. The Nobel Laureate brought it up a third time. Almost as if he realized the serious risks of looking only at the quantitative aspects, in the very last sentence, he warned us again: "We have not considered the first stage: the formation of the relevant beliefs on the basis of observation."

The man some consider one of the fathers of today's quantitative revolution told us several times that everything we might do with numbers is related to our beliefs. This turns out to be supremely important not only for all the obvious reasons but from neuroscientific ones as well.

Predisposed

None of us like to admit it, but most of us see what we want to.

As I just mentioned, we actually have to, otherwise the linear decisions of simple everyday life — never mind the "should I take that trade or not" — become too overwhelming.

If we learn nothing else from the debacle of 2008, let us accept the lesson that beliefs matter. When no one wanted to bid on a tranche of mortgages, it was because they believed, at least temporarily, that the price would go down, maybe to zero. Conversely, we got in that situation because hey, if you believe the value of homes will continue upward, then hey, give that mortgage. If you believe that people who have never consistently paid their bills will somehow start to, then hey, give them a chance to lose your money. After all, you can put together a model that shows that even if you are wrong on 20% of them, if you mix those assets in with mortgagees who have better credit, the risks will be offset.

In short, if you really want to measure your "risk," if you really want to know as much as possible about the odds of a trade or investment, then you better well keep your assumptions—which are beliefs—front and center. Skipping or forgetting about stage one adds risk!

Otherwise, the numbers will look you straight in the eye and lie—without a shred of guilt.

Accepting Our Responsibility for Judgment Calls

Now if three warnings about the role of the qualitative weren't enough, Markowitz actually went one step further and said: "Judgment should then be used … on the basis of factors or nuances not taken into account by the formal computations."

But wait, wasn't the whole idea to remove judgment, to remove any subjectivity and play a numbers game with the ultimate in numbers tools? Evidently not.

To judge means to assess and choose amongst scenarios of the future for which we can have only incomplete information. Markowitz clearly understood that despite his outsized contribution of calculable risk, certain details, "nuances" to use his words, defy being the objects of computation. And this, dear class, is what you need to understand—at least if you want to reduce the risks that inevitable and immeasurable uncertainty entail.

The bottom line is that, in general, we have abdicated our need to use the judgment demanded by a fundamentally uncertain situation under the illusion that the answer is always in the math.

Market performance emerges from owning the need to always be improving our judgment.

Chapter 4

Seeing What We Want but Missing the Obvious

Day 3: Special Lecture on a New Psychology of Risk
Chicago University

June 3, 2011

What About Our Ostensibly Irrational Behavior?

Picking up right where we left off last week, let's think about beliefs, judgment, and thinking itself. If we review the collective evidence, from both experience and science, we easily find that the subset of skills we focus on in school—the linear, deliberate, and often mathematically based analyses—has in effect been mistaken for our most intelligent dimension of thinking. I submit, however, that the obsession with 1600 or today's 2400 SAT scores has surreptitiously betrayed us.

To give a little perspective, or the context that is proving to be like the Dewey Decimal System of brain organization, two dominant veins of metacognition (thinking about thinking) weave their ideas through many many years of history. Early records indicate that even before Socrates, a man called Alcmaeon reportedly completed the first dissections on animals and discovered the optic nerve we all have connected to our brains. He correctly conjectured that our senses send information to the brain, which in turn uses the input to concoct a perception. In short, making judgments from the evidence of what we can see, hear, taste, and experience turns into the school known as empiricism.

Protagoras, obviously another of the Greek thinkers, theorized that indeed empiricism, the theory that all knowledge derives from our experiences as perceived through our senses, logically led to what my manager at IBM tried in vain, at least back then, to make me see—"perception is reality."

Contrast that with the school of rationalism, which for practical purposes says that our perceptions can fool us and we need the mental gymnastics of reason and logic in order to gain insight and wisdom. Aristotle for one didn't buy the perception argument and to pile on the argument for rationalism, Plato then deemed perception too ephemeral too mean much. Reasoning, therefore, could be the only viable method of understanding. Jump a few millennia ahead and the tradition of rationalism continued with Descartes and his famous saying, "I think therefore I am."

But what do these philosophies of thinking have to do with trading, you might be wondering?

It's not a far jump from the concept of rationalism to the economic concept of the rational man and his decisions based on the proper understanding of expected value.

Conversely, it is not a great leap from empiricism to the major tenet of today's latest search for how we really think and decide, that is, behavioral economics, the field that says we are indeed not rational or we wouldn't keep making the mistakes in probability judgment that seem to incinerate too many accounts of all sizes.

In other words, so the story goes, we can trust neither our beliefs nor our judgment—no matter what Markowitz said. Lab tests show that we don't pick the probabilistically correct choice; instead, we undervalue gains and overvalue losses, we place too much weight on recent events, etc.

The solution offered, however, dictates more of the same kind of thinking—the "rational" and probabilistically correct.

I will tell you what, gang. I don't buy it. I hesitate to take on the Establishment, particularly when part of it invited me here to give this lecture series, but really now, the problem seems to lie more in a form of laziness. Harry Markowitz said it would be difficult. He knew that like Freud at the turn of the previous century, he didn't have the tools (yet) to delve into what literally is a belief or a judgment or the psychological side of the matter, but that the pay dirt would be found there.

Markowitz hit the nail on the head—know your beliefs (which limit your scope) and figure out how to make better judgment calls. We've got the neuroscience now to know that beliefs provide an important element of the context, and fully exploiting the context provides the way to make the best judgment call.

Missing the Obvious

On the other hand, we have been strikingly irrational in not noticing one thing about ourselves.

In much of economics and psychology, we have been looking for the answers in only two of the three dimensions of the human mind and psyche—thought and behavior. This approach leaves a logical (or rational) gap no matter which way you prefer your metacognition! Clearly thinking and doing includes a third dimension—the much messier realm of how we feel when we are thinking or "behaving."

We "kinda-sorta" give credence to it in an abstract way. CNBC of late has cried out for animal spirits. We gauge sentiment with monthly research reports. We, or at least portfolio managers and traders at major banks, talk about confidence and conviction. But in the Ivory Towers where people who spend all of their time thinking about models of decisions, the focus remains mostly, although luckily not exclusively, on expected utility and emotion regulation, i.e., perceived value and emotion reduction. The assumptions about the superiority of our cognitive capacities are just that—assumptions.

Assembling data from multiple fields of neuroscience, however, demands that we realize we are more than our thoughts and our behaviors. We are in fact, mostly feeling beings.

The tenets of the cognitive "revolution"—triune models of the brain, neural doctrines, two different brain systems, a logical and an emotional one, are about to be faced with extinction.

For example, two weeks ago, we discussed the "it" factor in IBM's "Watson." Anyone care to remember what it was? *"Confidence?"* said Renee from her intentionally chosen seat one away from Michael.

Exactly!

And where in your being does confidence occur? Literally—is it a thought or a feeling? Is it a sense or an experience in your skull?

Watson, the *Jeopardy*-playing computer *simulated* full humanity, or what we feel via calculation. Yes, it is another technological feat for Watson to *comprehend* natural language the way that "he" does. But the point here is how much like a human he had to become to do it. Essentially, Watson needed to know what he believed and to make a judgment call based on an electronic form of the feeling of confidence. He won—yes. But if you really look at it, he did so because he could "know" that he "felt" confident much more quickly than his human competitors.

Who Has Been Looking the Other Way?

As it turns out, the historical schools of rationalism and empiricism *both* missed out on something that the philosopher Hume noticed, Darwin wrote about, Freud expanded upon, and now brain scientists are demonstrating. The missing ingredient combines a bit of both—observation that other factors are at work and the logical deduction that these factors may explain a lot, maybe even everything.

David Hume, the 19th-century philosopher, generally considered to be in the empirical camp, noticed it when he said that reason is subject to passion, or we think things are a certain way because we want them to be that way—a comment that almost predicts the now-demonstrated ambiguity aversion. Later, Darwin wrote a book called *The Expression of the Emotions in Man and Animals*. He described emotions as the source of beneficial actions. Fear and anger could lead a person to behave in a way that saved them from harm. Freud, arguably, combined empiricism and rationalism when he abandoned his *Project for a Scientific Psychology*—an explication of the neuroanatomy and chemistry of thoughts and feelings—and settled for the backward induction of deducing how people must be feeling from either their behavior or their distressing bodily symptoms.

And now neuroscience—in fact, a whole new world of neuroscience— is catching up. You often hear of the triune model of the brain, which says that the frontal cortex makes us human, the middle of the brain mediates emotion, and the base of the brain keeps your heart beating. The neuroscience vanguard, however, abandoned that concept a few years ago. The newest understanding states that perception occurs from snippets of activity *across* the brain; or that the brain works more in line with how the glia cells work, as we discussed in our previous lecture.

The Critical Context

This new knowledge of the brain logically matches what we are learning about context being crucial to everything from where the brain does math, to how language is interpreted, to assumptions about emotion. It runs parallel to the widely supported idea that "meaning" as identified through emotion, underlies decision making. If you think about it, the concept of the "background" broadcast of the 85% of your brain that is glia logically lines up with the empirical evidence for beliefs governing perception—if you are a quant, you believe in quant, or if you are a technical or fundamental analyst, you believe in your methods. And your beliefs implicitly include the emotion of confidence. Otherwise, you would doubt—and not believe—and look for another method!

In a brain that creates efficiency through the use of context, is not wanting to take another loss (emphasizing more recent experience) actually irrational, or is it conservative? Maybe a loss creates a context of fear, which would not be irrational, and in turn we become more cautious.

The problem stems not from hardwired tendencies to make poor judgment calls but instead from learned or mis-learned ideas about all of the dimensions of our psyches and how they fit together to create the contexts in which we think, analyze, and decide. Maybe we just need to learn to operate the machinery of our minds via a whole new user's manual.

Antonio Damasio, now widely considered one of the world's foremost neuroscientists, first brought this to the world's attention with an argument to counter the rationalists in his 1994 bestseller, *Descartes' Error*. He and his colleagues detailed numerous accounts of individuals who had sustained brain damage to areas of the brain known to be particularly important to the experience of emotion. After their injuries, these patients became completely unable to make even the simplest of decisions. One patient simply couldn't choose between two dates for an appointment, railing on for quite a long time about the benefits and liabilities of two different dates until, finally, Damasio just told him which date to come back. Others couldn't make a choice about which cereal to buy or what combination of clothing to wear in the morning.

The work contributed to, or re-ignited, two major ideas that had fallen by the wayside through the ages of rational, computer-like thinking about the human brain. One, it reconnected the whole system by noting that we feel emotion primarily in our bodies not in our heads. And second, when we can't feel, much of who we are or can be disappears. Damasio correctly asserted the famous saying should be: "I feel therefore I am."

In fact, while unfortunately Wall Street has gone about its business in ignorance of the centrality of emotion, a few more bold scientists, with their eyes wide open, sought to further the discussion about thinking and emotion. And guess what? Every day more research proves that not only are emotions *not* something to be shunned, dismissed, or overridden, but we need them for meaning, we need them for vision, and we use them for essentially everything. We might be able to resolve an equation without being attached to it, but if we didn't *want* the answer for some other reason, why would we?

Therefore, ironically, the last thing you want is no emotion!

We can't actually apply math or logic, let alone do other analyses, make judgments, or decisions, if we lack feeling and emotion.

If A therefore depends on B, then how can B be inferior to A? Thinking it is, is ironically and exactly illogical!

Your Brain "On Risk": Neuroeconomics and Neuroemotion

Neuroeconomics specifically studies the brain-making economic decisions. In 2005, a great article ran in the *Journal of Economic Literature*. Titled "Neuroeconomics: How Neuroscience Can Inform Economics," the article's authors made the point over and over:

> "It is not enough to 'know' what should be done; it is also necessary to 'feel' it" and "to influence behavior, the cognitive system must operate via the affective system." (Affect being the academic word for emotion).

These two sentences, by the way, ultimately encompass everything you need to know about the psychology of decision making under uncertainty. Think about it—if it is not enough to simply know and a feeling must be had to act, then every act has a feeling substrate, and all you really need to do is know what it is to do more of what you want.

And then, like Markowitz harkening back to his stage one of beliefs, they rephrased their point again: "We are only now beginning to appreciate the importance of affect for normal decision making."

Having drawn their own four-quadrant model of the mind where the first quadrant is that linear deliberate SAT-acing–type thinking, they also surmise how so many of us might have missed this: "*Since quadrant 1 often does not have conscious access to activity in the other quadrants, it is perhaps not surprising that it tends to over-attribute behavior to itself—i.e., to deliberate decision processes.*"

But be forewarned.

It gets worse—or better—depending on your vantage point. Those dedicated to the cause of probabilistic rationalism took another hit two years later with an article entitled, "Being Emotional During Decision Making—Good or Bad? An Empirical Investigation." Underscoring the radical drift of what our aforementioned team deemed "Radical Neuroeconomics," these scientists stated:

> *Contrary to the popular belief that feelings are generally bad for decision making, we found that individuals who experienced more intense feelings had higher decision-making performance....*
>
> *Individuals who were better able to identify and distinguish among their current feelings achieved higher decision-making performance....*
>
> *This study suggests that whether their feelings are actually beneficial or harmful to decisions may largely depend upon how people experience, treat and use their feelings during decision making.*

This is the emotions-as-data school that my company uses as our foundation of improving the performance and decision-making skills of traders, C-suiters, and athletes. But in the meantime, can anyone tell me why with this kind of science now becoming very old news, HSBC still pays for newspaper ads saying, "Never let emotions cloud your judgment" and deeming it "textbook financial advice"?

Michael chuckled. He had to admit he was becoming a convert to this new psychology of uncertainty and couldn't help but answer, "Well, as their behavior and your logic has explained, banks aren't exactly spending any time thinking about anything other than formulas now, are they?"

I guess that is the point, isn't it, Michael? It may be textbook (or otherwise I wouldn't be here giving this lecture, would I?), but that doesn't make it good advice. If HSBC or any other broker could literally remove emotions from their clients' judgments, they would be very sorry. As no decisions would be made at all, no commission revenue would be gained.

The New Psychology of Risk and Uncertainty: Lecture Summary and Your Key

Over the course of these past few Friday afternoons, we've covered the following points:

Despite our desire, we can never know for sure what will happen tomorrow.

Probabilities tell us something but not everything we would like to, or need to, know.

Deciding how to divide up a pot of cash should be done only after one explicitly knows what they believe and why they believe it.

Even then, at the end of the day, judgment will come into play.

Judgment requires emotion. (Don't think you aren't using it.)

So here's the challenge. Watson the computer may have been able to "enumerate" confidence, but in the reality of human markets and humans making both market and model decisions, that isn't the way it goes. We might be able to learn to systematically analyze *our internal* confidence levels and we can certainly change our processes so that we become systematic about the qualitative; but so far, very few people on Wall Street, no matter what their rank, have done it.

On the day of the Flash Crash in May 2010, certain traders used not their models but their brains, their memories, and their pattern recognition skills to immediately decide to shut down their automatic trading systems. They judged something to be awry. They didn't know what; but in effect, their lack of confidence or what could also be called that dreaded word "fear" served as their best risk manager.

That is exactly how Darwin said it was supposed to work—an emotion like fear could be useful. As it turns out, that famous saying, "The only thing we have to fear is fear itself" is another mistake.

In fact, the only true thing we have to fear, at least when it comes to decision about uncertainty, is a complete lack of fear.

To trade or make any decision under the auspices of uncertainty, one should always explicitly know where they stand on the spectrum of fear to confidence. If they do, they have a shot at knowing their preexisting conditions of beliefs and, in turn, at making their best judgment call. I challenge you, as you leave this lecture, to devise for yourselves the self-awareness and tracking systems that will indeed allow you to do so. If you do, you can be confident that you'll be honoring the wisdom of the ages as well as the working in concert with your entire suite of mental faculties. Ultimately, this strategy paves the way to to knowing the difference between a plethora of different types of feelings, intuition and impulse, being two that everyone would like to be facile with.

In turn, and most importantly, you will always live to trade another day!

PART 2

GETTING THE RIGHT GLASSES FOR BETTER MARKET VISION

Chapter 5

Rolling Out of the Midwest Back to Wall Street

As Michael finished packing up his U-Haul, he almost couldn't believe he was leaving Chicago for New York—again! After his first foray at Schoenberg Trading, he never had really expected to go back. He certainly hadn't foreseen landing on a desk at a top bank. He sure hoped he wasn't driving toward a siren song. The markets had changed since the Internet boom and bust. Computers and algorithms drove so much more volume now. Maybe instead of hoping to manage money, he should just be developing models. He certainly had the math cred even if he lacked the desire.

On the plus side, looking at it through a psychological lens seemed promising. When he first heard Denise Shull's guest lecture, he had to grapple with it. He understood her logic—the limits of numbers, the role of beliefs and judgment, and the idea of conscious emotion as part of the context in a decision. Nevertheless, he still could feel how, despite his intrigue, tangible numbers sounded inordinately easier!

His new "friend" Renee on the other hand didn't see the problem. Ironically, she had turned out to know a whole lot more about trading than he would have ever guessed. When he originally had called her about the special lecture, she had blown him away with not only being one of the organizers but with also being a bit of an options trader herself. Even more amazing was the revelation that her father traded on the floors of the Chicago Board Options Exchange and the Chicago Mercantile Exchange. "He always said the numbers only take you so far and then there is a leap," she said. "It's a leap that is about reading the other people and about the feelings of fear or confidence you have in that read."

According to her, her father, Christopher, had "made money in all kinds of markets but he never could fully explain why (or how). In truth," she said, "that's mostly what got me so interested in psychology."

She explained that he was also one of the few to make it when he switched from the floor to the screen. "Most don't, but he ported whatever it is without too much trouble. I want to know why some traders have a knack and some have to struggle and some just never get it. I want to know what makes a great trader—from the point of view of their whole psyches—body, brain, and mind! What was it that was special about my father?"

The subject of beliefs in particular got her going. She insisted they formed a foundation and, almost no matter what they were, skewed the believer's perception. Her favorite example of beliefs and perception was what she called her great water-skiing "misadventure."

Late on a Friday afternoon in Cocoa Beach, she and two friends had gone water skiing. Unfortunately, the boat had a tiny engine and Renee had trouble getting out of the water on one ski. They decided, given that no one was around, to use the easier tactic of her dropping one ski once she was out of the water. It worked until her friend thought she wanted to slow down and and inadvertently caused her to fall. Figuring that they should grab the ski from the darkening water where they left it as soon as possible, they let Renee bobb in the water as they circled the boat around. They had skied at sunset scores of times and normally this ritual would only take a minute or so. But the Banana River's current was surprisingly swift, and within moments her friends were not only completely out of sight and but also out of shouting range. When they didn't return within three or four minutes and she couldn't see them anywhere on the water, she distressingly intuited that the boat's engine had failed. Earlier, while putting on her skis in the water, she had heard her friend Zap curse as he had to turn the key a couple of times to get the engine running. With a palpable panic she knew she was completely alone in the water. The sun was setting fast, and she was quite sure her friends were floating downriver. She simply had no choice but to swim in. She pointed herself northeast toward a Lobster sign on shore and did a kind of side stroke in order to hold onto her ski. Yet, she quickly "realized" that at very best, she was only keeping pace with the current. She would swim for what she estimated as five minutes and then look up to see where she was vis-à-vis a hotel perpendicular to her position. After a few of these five-minute intervals, she seemed to actually be farther south of the hotel! Stopping more than a few times to save energy and to assess her worsening circumstances, she eventually noticed a white sailboat anchored a ways off-shore. With the sun now completely down and the river lit with bright moonlight, the white of the boat attracted light like a neon dress under a 1970's style black light. Within moments of changing direction yet again and pointing herself towards this beacon instead of towards the shore, she surprisingly realized she was finally making good time. As she drew nearer and nearer to her new goal, she marveled at how previously she couldn't seem to make any progress but when a clear objective appeared, she started making quick progress—despite, at this point, having been in the water close to two hours.

As it turned out, however, her friends had ultimately anchored the broken boat and also swam in—but within the context of a radically different set of perceptions and beliefs. They never experienced what turned out to be her false perception of making no progress. They knew they were moving farther and farther from their reference point because they could more easily see how far from it they had swum. With Renee's initial navigational sign being a much more distant neon sign and a building on shore, her perception and her beliefs had been way off base. She had been making forward progress the whole time. Most likely, she had been swimming more or less in the direction of the sailboat the whole time and it was simple distance and being at water level that prevented her from seeing it until the moon came up. Had she just kept swimming in her original direction when she first started she would have made it all the way back not only to shore but to her friend's dock without having spent an extra hour and a half in the water! Instead, she had stopped, reassessed, and headed toward different landmarks six or seven times before spotting the "lighthouse" of the white sailboat.

As she relayed to Michael, "My belief that I wasn't making any progress (even though I was) meant everything to the repeatedly incorrect assessments and decisions I made. The incorrect belief stemmed from a skewed perception, but I didn't know it—despite my repeated attempts to accurately analyze what was happening."

He understood, particularly in the case of swimming in the dark, but he disagreed that there was virtually no such thing as complete objectivity. After all, everyone sees and studies through a lens or a context that comes kind of "pre-packaged."

There was also the matter of emotion. *Everyone* on Wall Street says, "Control your emotions." How do people reconcile needing emotions and controlling them at the same time? Michael's mother, the divorcee who went back to get her own PhD in cognitive psychology, always said the research showed you could regulate—and really, isn't that the same as control?—your emotions with your thoughts.

But Shull seemed to be saying in the lectures that the research unequivocally proved that you almost couldn't think without emotion. Emotion gives meaning; and without meaning, how does one ever "know" anything? The two clearly conflict. Which is it—rely on or regulate?

Floor Traders, Flash Crashes, and Flirtations

At one point, near the Ohio border, Michael's mind flashed back to a discussion he had been lucky enough to have with Renee's father,

Christopher. Renee's parents had hosted what turned out to be a sublime graduation party for her at Topolobampo (the restaurant where President Obama turns up now and then), and Michael had fortuitously found himself on the guest list. When Christopher discovered that Michael was headed for a trader training program at a major bank, he had explained his own retirement from the exchange as being directly attributable to it being much harder to read the other players from what he called "upstairs."

"Not impossible on the screen," he said, "but a lot harder than when I could see the whites of another trader's eyes across the pit." A new skill for an old dog that wasn't sure he needed to learn it, was the way he put it.

Michael wondered, have the markets changed so much that he wouldn't recognize them either? Had HFT (high-frequency trading) turned them into a whole new ballgame? Will the only way to do it be via models, which only approximate, and algorithms? Will in the end this job amount to being a robotic arm operator? He has been assured it wouldn't be in the interview.

But then he wondered, how does the human interact with the computer? Are the old changes in speed and rhythms—the tape reading that he was taught at Schoenberg—still even there?

And then he remembered a study that he had brought up in the interview. He had just stumbled on it on Physorg.com. The gist was that the best market simulation model developed to date relied on "sentiment" of various market participants. Reported by a group of Italian academics, this artificial market demonstrated "sentiment" flowing from one type of market participant to another.

In doing so, this market model ended up looking the most like actual market data, where big moves beget more big moves and, in probability terms, the less likely events or "behaviors" were indeed more common. When plotted on probability graphs, the curve has the "fat tails" or more time spent in theoretically unlikely events—exactly as real markets have proven to unfold. Discussing this study, in fact, seemed to be what clinched the new job for him. The managing director on one of the desks had seemed quite leery of hiring a new trader who had a PhD. Normally, people like that went into research and built models. They didn't sit on trading desks and deal with the much messier world of gyrating markets.

One thing Michael did know for sure: in a practical way, all prices emerged from perception and perceptions change. One day a few years ago, a condo on Chicago's Gold Coast sold for $1.5 million; and a few short months and a market crash later, the one next door sat on the market priced at $1.1 million. Now, you could grab it for a mere $850,000! What had changed? The building was just as beautiful and well located as ever. It was how people thought about the value that changed the price—both when it was going up and when it was coming back down.

The study seemed to say that tracing the trail of market players' thoughts and feelings from one trader or investor to another held the key to creating a research tool that looked like real markets. Surely, one could use computers to help with this and, even more surely, given that humans built all the models anyway, couldn't it be a matter of learning a new, albeit still fundamentally, human game?

The Long Black Line of US Highway 80

As the seemingly interminable road across Pennsylvania just kept on painting a long straight black line in front of him, Michael's mind wandered. He and Renee definitely were not "an item"; but looking from the outside in, one might not know that. Somehow, before he had left Chicago, they kept finding themselves biking to her volleyball matches on Oak Street Beach or sitting in Starbucks discussing the differences between classic decision theory, subjective probability, and emotion neuroscience.

All he could think of was how it seemed every time his feelings got strong enough for him to notice, if he paid attention to them, he inevitably did something he regretted. She lobbied for the idea that emotions made meaning—literally in the brain—and the fact that one could feel something but not act on it. She had a point in that certainly that had been his M.O. with her. To his knowledge, he had disguised even the slightest clue regarding the extent of his interest in her. He knew how he felt, but he didn't act on it. He hoped she might be doing the same. Maybe....

The End of a Long Summer

Stearnsmann Bank ranked within the top five of global banks and was known for their aggressive and comprehensive approaches to trading their own capital. They used both discretionary and automated trading across every market. New hire training had begun on Tuesday, July 5.

Every day for weeks now, Michael had sat in a chair for the better part of nine hours. He knew his days of academia's flexible schedules were over and he felt more than ready to get onto the desk and be in the action. Lectures on company policies, dealing with the media (did journalists ever call the junior guy?), the bank's proprietary market quotes and order-routing technology, and war stories from managing directors in each market—US equities, emerging markets, US "govvies," currencies—were necessary.

Despite his antsiness, he had gained the basics of what he needed to know to not be a complete imbecile on his (second) first day out on the trading floor. The research and quantitative analyses segment even let him show off just a tad with a few nuanced questions. New York's legendary summer humidity permeated the building and his mind fast-forwarded a few days to the class's "graduation dinner" in the Grill Room of one of the Wall Street power brokers' favorite places, the Four Seasons Restaurant.

As he walked into today's class a moment late (due to the huge number of people buying frappuccinos), he heard, "Who will put in the first bid? $100 for.... Do I hear 50?" His fellow classmates were bidding it up fast. "Do I hear 80? 85? 90?"

Michael didn't hesitate. "95!" he shouted. He figured the iced quad latte that had made him a moment late was now free. Then he heard that guy from MIT bid 100 and wondered why everyone giggled?

"Michael, unless you bid 105, you have to pay him 95," his new buddy Bill explained with a smirk. "That's what you get for walking in late, chump! The second highest bidder pays their bid amount!"

Aside from his embarrassment in front of the class, he couldn't believe he hadn't noticed that Denise Shull from the campus lecture was today's guest lecturer.

Chapter 6

Do You Need to Be Psychic to Deal With Uncertainty?

Stearnsmann Bank New Hire Training
Day 1: Market, Risk, and Trading Psychology Lecture

July 28, 2011

Denise Shull
On the screen, Michael saw these words:

> *No matter how you analyze a market or a trade, no matter what your timeframe, the only "thing" you are ever trying to deduce is if other market players will value the asset in question differently in the future.*

Winning a Beauty Contest

Bill's right, Michael, you didn't know it, but you weren't simply bidding for the $100 bill. In fact, you were playing a slightly modified version of the 1930's newspaper beauty contest game that John Maynard Keynes used as an example for the correct thought process of investing and trading in his classic economics book, *The General Theory.*

You see, before there were the Flash Crashes of 2010 and the mass crashes of 2008, 2001, and 1987, before there was a "Battle of the Quants" conference series, and even before the Nobel Laureate Harry Markowitz first fully applied mathematics to the calculation of risk, Keynes pointed out the most fundamental truth of markets and trading that remains in place today. He showed how winning the market game required invoking the same process one should go through in order to win the beauty contests that were then posted in the newspapers of Keynes' day.

Just as the current media do with their provocative opinion-based journalism strategies intended to garner viewership, various newspapers had begun publishing beauty contests using photographs and write-in voting to boost circulation. Typically 100 pictures appeared and six were chosen by the readership. Eventually the women themselves who were voted to be the most beautiful ended up in Atlantic City for the "Fall Frolic," but readers could also win by picking the six that would win the most votes. Everyone could win.

Keynes point was that this newspaper premonition of *American Idol* provided an object lesson for successful trading and investing. It wasn't about picking the one you thought possessed the greatest beauty, although that seemed on the surface as the obvious thing to do. The way to win, if you were the average player sitting at home, was to choose the women other voters were most likely to pick.

> *It is not a case of choosing those [faces] that, to the best of one's judgment, are really the prettiest, nor even those that average opinion genuinely thinks the prettiest. We have reached the third degree where we devote our intelligences to anticipating what average opinion expects the average opinion to be.*

He actually described his strategy as not one derivation but two whole steps removed from what the contest appeared to be. This carries the trading analogy through. In market games, it isn't your opinion that counts nor even the immediate opinions of others' opinions of whatever asset you are trading. Winning the market game means that you need to deduce what the perception of others will be about, for example, GE or GOOG in the future.

Unfortunately, Michael, in our object lesson here, there is almost no way to win. You can play for the fun of it but you have to realize that the only risk management strategy that doesn't get you into trouble is to be the third highest bidder as the bids get within striking range of "fundamental value." Just like in trading, where you want to exit when the momentum really picks up, if you bid no higher than $80 or $85, most likely someone else will think there is still $15 to $20 of "undervalue" in this stock. "Hell, I'll pay $90 for $100," they decide, and then some naïve bystander who doesn't understand the real game jumps in at $95 on the same basic logic.

For some reason, people get focused as $100 approaches, and the rules become clear at this point. Instantaneously, everyone remembers or realizes that the only way out of paying $90 becomes to bid $100, and then the only way out for you, Michael, of paying $95 is to bid $105.

They use this game at Harvard's behavioral finance executive class, and I've been told of the auction ending with numbers like $120 or $130, which, frankly, reminds me of what happens in a "short squeeze." In fact, the short-squeeze lesson brings this exercise home. Short squeezes present an easy place to see Keynes' reality. You can lose lots of money fast if you are caught in one and, over the long haul, remembering that just because *you* think something is highly *overvalued* doesn't mean everyone else isn't in the throes of the fear of missing out and therefore continue to try to buy the rapidly rising stock (or gold future or whatever). I myself had an instance, in 2004, where my broker's research showed someone's technology to be ineffective but their marketing continued to be so good that the stock just kept on going up. I finally gave in for a big loss and I still see that ticker on CNBC at around my original entry point. In other words, so much for my opinion and for the opinion one removed from me — it was the opinions in the third degree that counted more than anything!

We go about making our market decisions based on facts we try to find but, in the end, they don't tell us what we want and need to know. Facts can never be more than clues in a puzzle. We, if we are going to consistently get it more right than wrong, need the explicit strategy of predicting people.

The Irreducible Truth of Speculation

You make money by correctly predicting the opponent's future perception—not "the facts"!

Now I know this reality doesn't go down easy. Every one of you just spent a boatload of money, time, and energy getting graduate-level degrees from top institutions. You have been training to get good at facts, and I am here to tell you that you might be better off studying to be a psychic.

It's not that the facts, or what are likely to be the future facts, have no value at all. But they have to be put in the proper context. When will other people know the same thing? When will they see it? What other factors will obscure the truth from being widely known?

Answers to these types of questions can't be black and white. Regardless, you need to be thinking about how the future will play out in other traders' minds. Remembering that in the end, this is all that counts. Thinking "socially" also puts your brain in the right frame of mind to make the best judgment calls. It gets you in tune with the real game.

Question in the back of the room? Yes?

"But what about the fact that so much of today's trading stems from algorithms executing on models, and no human really is involved?" asked a guy who had just graduated from MIT's financial engineering program.

Yes, I get that question over and over. But think about it, where did the model and the algo come from in the first place? Sure, we have some rudimentary true machine learning now; but even behind, in a market context, some human somewhere made decisions about implied volatility and assumptions about other factors that they can and frankly often do change. It's called "recalibrating the model" and it goes on on a regular basis.

In other words, the models behind the matrix of electrons began as perceptions and clusters of ideas in human minds. Hence, no matter how computationally complex, cash flow fundamental, technical, or esoteric your analyses are, you still are searching for one thing: *Why* will anyone pay a different price in the future than you are paying now?

What does the price, any price, of a stock, future, or tradable bond really actually mean anyway?

Take the price of AAPL today. What does it tell you? At any given moment, doesn't it simply reflect the net perception of the value of Apple as a company? Actually, does the price of the stock reflect market players' views of the value of the company today or does it reflect their view of the value of where the stock might be trading at tomorrow? Or wait, there is even another possibility. Does the price simply communicate that more people believe Apple Inc. will make more money next year than they did last year? We can go one—right after great earning you might see a pop in the price—"Wow, everyone is buying iPads"—but wait … if everyone is buying them now, who will be left to buy next year? Maybe their revenues will decrease.

Price reflects perception, and perceptions can stem from almost innumerable combinations of factors.

Market numbers, therefore, differ as a category from other kinds of numbers such as arithmetic or algebraic numbers. The trading price of AAPL or a 10-year Treasury only ever conveys the collective but relatively momentary judgment call of everyone participating in that market at that moment. A market number contains nothing precise or absolute in and of itself.

Furthermore, the saying "that's what makes a market" comes into play here in that you've always got to have a buyer and seller, right? In a pure world, it's logical to assume that buyers buy because they think the price is going higher and sellers sell because they think it is going lower. Sure, there are forced buys and sells that impact the market, particularly when it moves in one direction over a relatively short period of time; but generally speaking, we can accept that transactions have two parties with mostly opposite perspectives.

Therefore, a single, very underappreciated, fluid, and elusive force prints each and every price to the tape—the joint perception, *for whatever reasons*, of two human beings or the algorithms they control. Because the number by definition quantifies the perception, it appears orders of magnitude more factual than it is.

Every single price at every single moment now and forever will be only a perception—nothing more and nothing less.

To make matters even more perceptual and less precise, the numbers change every nanosecond. Give them a whole day and they may change quite dramatically. A whole month, year, or decade and who knows if 100 means 100 or if it means 500 or 1? Prices really are a bit like all of those people in all of those cities all over the world who say. "Don't like our weather? Stick around an hour, it will change."

Truth only partially exists in stocks when a company goes bankrupt and their stock goes to zero. Aside from that, whether AAPL goes higher or IBM goes lower in and of itself tricks us into thinking we are playing a numbers game. Even the common term "expected value" in statistics gets glossed over. We focus on the value part and not the expected part. Expectations are simply that, what we think will happen—but certainly, unless you are an extremely talented psychic, not what will actually happen!

At the moment of an IPO or merger, something akin to a truth may also fleetingly exist. But what happens when trading starts the next day? If nothing else, the fact that the next buyer or seller can bid higher or sell lower, for whatever reason they may have—perceived value, need to raise cash, or for want of a manipulated perception created for other market participants—proves that "truth" simply does not exist. What if a news story or a no-bid situation in one corner of the market causes a reaction and a selling or buying wave moves quickly through other markets? When prices are down, you can argue that they are undervalued or you can argue that the trend is down and prices tend to keep going in the direction they are going.

Finally, what about the ever-present trading question of "what if I just hold onto it a little bit longer?" The essentially infinite number of choices when it comes to the question of how much longer to hang onto a trade means, by definition, certainty and truth cannot exist.

It might seem like I am beating a dead horse here. Yet I know that in the back of your minds, this imprecise business of perception goes against the grain of almost everything you learned in school. It gets said without anyone actually saying it—somewhere there is a mysterious formula for the truth in the market and all assets traded on one. We semiconsciously keep looking for it and that is a waste of time—time which can be better spent putting our numbers into the proper context.

The Right Role for Numbers

I'm not saying that mathematically based analyses should be thrown out. I don't mean that at all!

However, the math we do should have the right purpose, and you shouldn't mistake models for truth when they are only a clue to the real question.

If the real question is, "What will other player's perceive in the future?", then quantitative analyses make sense in their right context—as clues but not as answers.

From my perspective this remains the proverbial elephant in the room even today with all the post-crash talk of irrational behavior. Markets serve many functions in the overall economic picture but their actual operation, the waves that move the numbers in one direction or another are more social (and by that I mean the perceptual waves that travel from market player to market player) than anything else.

For example, the fear of missing out or not getting the trade the other guy got plays a huge role. It's part of something called "regret theory"—a particular type of academic decision model that factors in the role of regret or, more importantly, the prospect of regret. The potential for regret drives prices in ways much more profoundly than generally recognized, particularly in bubbles and upward pushes.

Call it Shull's "social market hypothesis," if you like, but remember, this game remains messy and imprecise and political and variable—an endless poker game where even the cards don't have clear values. Internalizing this truth and organizing your market strategies around it automatically puts you in the very desirable "one-up" competitive position against those who continue to fiddle with numbers while not understanding the essence of the game.

Now, obviously, trading couldn't occur without numbers. We can't completely ignore them if for no other reason than we need higher ones than we had before to be making any money.

But the process for growing bigger numbers differs from what it seems. Think of it this way: our lives happen via our bodies, but our bodies alone are not our lives. Transportation happens via trains, planes, and automobiles, but the trip isn't the plane. In each case, the "container" (the human body or the plane) is the envelope, the transport mechanism, the vehicle. The end goal, however, exists beyond the mechanism.

Likewise, when it comes to markets: *numbers actually serve a whole different master—a master less precise, more artful, and much more subject to interpretation—the function of a language.*

Languages, even those based on the same structure as American, British, and Chinese English, convey or attempt to convey meaning from one individual to another. The same word in two dialects might mean something completely different; ditto for the same word in two different contexts. Take the word "fixture," for example. If you live in the United States, you most likely think bathroom faucet. If you live in England, you hear the word fixture and immediately think about the schedule of your favorite football team.

Words never amount to more than subjective symbols. Symbols deliver a meaning but they exist to refer to something else and inherently have none of the intrinsic or immutable law of 2 plus 2 equals 4.

Solving the eternal puzzle of markets depends entirely on your ability to fluidly wield the sword of numbers as a language and not as a law.

Mistakenly co-opting numbers' language role into investigative formulas intended to discover some definitive answer contributes directly to financial mayhem at every level. It misleads us into thinking we have indeed managed the risk of the numbers deflating on us. It tricks us into believing that we know what the future will bring.

Think of it this way. If the numbers in the market's case serve only as breadcrumbs to the real answer (other players' future perception), it makes no sense to focus all of our intellectual firepower on the bread (wheat, rye, or pumpernickel). We need to think in terms of why the crumbs of clues are developing in the way that they are.

The Gaping Hole in Today's Risk Management

The optimal risk management would put quantitative analyses in the proper *qualitative contexts* to deduce their real meaning. Had this kind of qualitative, interpretive language perspective been in place in the years preceding 2008, then the anecdotal accounts of the fairly widespread fear and anxiety may well have had a shot at being heeded.

Instead, back in 2008, what you had were assets that were making money right up until they weren't, only a few players to trade in them, and then a fast-spreading rumor that the music was about to stop. But if a common sense context, instead of the alchemy of mixed credit classes, had been able to even get a seat at the table, then more players might have been on the short side. If more people had been shorting those complex credit instruments, the demand would have been mitigated and most likely so would have the price. Had that happened, the billion- and trillion-dollar bonfires might not have been quite so dramatic.

This holds true for any market decision. People who got annihilated buying the first dip when the Internet bubble cracked could be told the same thing. Ditto for the people who shorted it in 1999 when it had a year and a blow-off top to go. And certainly double-ditto for the people who could have looked past the relatively mundane returns of Bernie Madoff. Systematically checking for the human or social perception context would have led to wider awareness and less acting out of the insidious fear of missing out that pervades the trading mind.

Know that you are trading or investing against people who at the end of the day read the same books you do. You want for people to see what you do—just after you do. You don't need to know what everyone is doing, you only need to imagine that the people you are buying from or selling to are indeed more like you than you tend to think.

Traders get scared that they have to find something no one else knows. They worry that Goldman Sachs controls the whole market. Trust me, I know traders at Goldman and at plenty of other major institutions; they are actually human and they don't have some exclusive information unknown to the general population. They do, however, think in terms of social markets whether they realize it or not. In fact, in my experience, the better the trader, the more they think in terms of the human perception waves that certainly drive short-term markets. Regardless of any day's market rhythm, their thoughts naturally gravitate first toward how the price action is being perceived by their direct trading competitors.

Understanding Other Humans Isn't as Hard as It May Appear

Each of us has the skill to understand others in at least two specific ways: directly, when we can see another human being's physical movements and indirectly through symbols, when we can only see reflections or artifacts of their activity. Research shows that the brain uses a different system when it looks for people in symbols versus when it can see the actual person, but everyone's got both systems. Some of us use them better than others and that alone may explain "natural born traders," but we also can all get better at using what comes naturally.

Think about it. We all have to predict what other people are going to do almost every moment of our lives. Scientists call this mental ability "theory of mind," or ToM for short. It simply means consciously (or usually unconsciously) working with a theory of what is going on in someone else's head. In short, it is pattern recognition of likely human behavior.

We can see it most easily in any kind of navigating down a street or highway to get somewhere. For example, here in New York City, we do it walking down Lexington Avenue in particular. As some of you are new to New York, let me explain that Lex bisects the Upper East Side and in order to get anywhere you simply have no choice but to dodge and weave through the delivery people, the doyennes of Park Avenue, and the typical tourists trying to figure out which restaurant is and which isn't an authentic local joint. Outside of New York, everyone does it when they drive, otherwise every non-showroom car anywhere would be dent laden! In other words, we, essentially without much conscious thought, take in the scene and infer what others will do next. If we weren't all doing this as we go about our business, we'd all be running into each other much more often than we do!

But here's the good news, something I have been talking about since 2008 at least. This natural ability that we all have showed up in a groundbreaking study as the key to accurately reading markets. Called "Exploring the Nature of 'Trader Intuition'," the work showed (in the lead author Antoine Bruguier's words): "We find that skill in predicting price changes in markets with insiders correlates with scores on two ToM tests."

Now, if there is only one thing I don't need to educate you all on, it is statistical correlation. I can assure you, however, that this author didn't use the word incorrectly or lightly. Finished as part of a PhD program at the respected research school of California Institute of Technology, the paper also went through multiple reviews by the prestigious *Journal of Finance*, where it appeared last October. But some of you may be a bit worried about the term "insiders." No, it doesn't mean Raj Rajaratnam, although clearly when anyone pursues inside information they are indeed directly pursuing a social markets strategy. In this case, the term "insiders" refers to players in an artificial market who traded in that market with a more detailed understanding of the dividend payout scenarios. That understanding caused them to trade their experimental assets in a slightly different way, but the important part comes when completely uninformed players in the next phase of the experiment were asked to detect whether there was effectively intentional buying or selling.

In the second part of the experiment, some players could see the purposeful price movement and some couldn't. They were all playing while an fMRI machine recorded images of their brains. Researchers could then infer what kind of thinking was going on from what parts of the brain were being more heavily taxed. Each participant pushed a button each time they saw what they thought was purposeful buying (and, in fact, they also paid a small penalty if they missed it in order to keep their attention).

The team found that "increased activation" occurred in areas of the brain known to be key to theory of mind skills when the artificial market data had informed buyers and sellers in it versus when it did not.

But here's the real kicker of this particular experiment: the parts of the brain typically associated with formal mathematical thinking showed essentially not much at all going on!

Now I realize that this result could be a tad disconcerting, but I am confident, that with the training and resulting skills this group has, you will be able to capitalize on your natural theory of mind skills and put your entire mathematical prowess to better work—when you do so in the right context of trading other people's current and future perceptions (even if instantiated through computer models and algorithms).

Real Traders Predicting Real Markets

Does anyone here happen to recall seeing or reading the issue of *Vanity Fair* magazine that was out last summer, the one with a very young and beautiful Elizabeth Taylor on the cover? Now I know you all probably don't put *Vanity Fair* at the top of your regular reading lists but this one also highlighted an article about a very well-known (albeit normally very private) trader who clearly has got it down when it comes to reading markets as people's perceptions and not as numerical truths.

The article described Stevie Cohen, a nine-time repeat member of *Absolute Return* magazine's "The Rich List" (which has been running 10 years), who has been described as having a "Rain Man"–like gift for reading stock tickers. Gary Goldrin, formerly the CEO of his clearing firm, was quoted as saying: "I've seen all his records, hundreds of thousands of trades, all of it, and my conclusion is simply that the guy is an artist. He looks at a stock market in chaos and sees order. He was just right over and over and over."

I know the SEC is currently snooping around his offices but even if they were to find something not right, it doesn't change Cohen's legendary ability. Reportedly, beginning in the spring of his ninth-grade year and continuing right through college at the University of Pennsylvania, Cohen "did far better at the poker table than in the classroom." So he graduated to the windows in front of the Philadelphia Merrill Lynch window to "watch a stock go by at say, 50 … 50 … 50 … 50 …. And then it might go up or down a tick. You could see the trade happening. You could just watch it in slow motion. And later, not right away, I found I was pretty good at guessing which way those numbers would go…. There's kind of an art to reading the tape. I can't really explain it: It's about pattern recognition."

Bruguier's study explains it, at least in my opinion. For whatever reason, and maybe someday we will find out, Cohen clearly has well-honed people-reading skills—even if he doesn't know it. The question of natural-born traders gets asked over and over and over, and I think we really do have our answer in this research about leveraging one's theory of mind abilities versus relying on what we can see through the masquerade costume of a numbers game.

I am sure you all know that almost a century earlier, Jesse Livermore, memorialized in the book, *Reminiscences of a Stock Operator*, said essentially the exact same thing. Originally published in 1923, ostensibly as a report of a series of interviews with the legendary stock picker, the book indicates him to say "interested in the behavior of prices ... I could remember in detail how the prices had acted on the previous day, just before they went up or down.... A battle goes on in the stock market and the tape is your telescope."

Actually, my original trading mentor, Don Winton, had a similar talent too. When I first began trading, we would sit watching a spreadsheet of quotes flashing. We could see the bid price, the offer price, the last trade, and the supposed amount of stock available for sale and being bid for. The numbers would flash, just like Cohen says, and Don would say, "It's going up" (usually when I thought it was going down!), and I would say, "How do you know?", and he would say, "Just watch. Can't you see there are buyers?" Another guy we traded with, Eddie, always talked the same way: "they are buying or here they come to sell."

I realized one day that everyone I knew who could make a lot of money on a regular basis talked about the markets in terms of people. Think of the best market players you know, whether they run a billion dollar hedge fund or trade their own capital. If you listen over their shoulders you hear them speak to the screens as if the monitors can hear. Implicitly, their perceptions are not about the bars, lines, and formulas, but about the people behind the flashing electrons.

Anthropologists term it anthropomorphizing, or giving human qualities to non-human objects—but of course that would be wrong. I actually thought that at the time. Being right out of graduate school I kind of thought they were taking this numbers puzzle (yes, I admit it) and trying to turn it into something it wasn't. Then it hit me—in the case of reading markets, it wasn't infusing something non-human with humanity, it was simply seeing it for the truth it is.

In fact, when he wasn't around and I wasn't intimidated by Don's book-like reading of the market, I found that in fact I could do it, too. The owner of our trading firm, a gentleman named Robert Kanter, told me I had the best instincts he had ever seen after I had shown him the charts on a series of drug stocks on a Friday; and on Monday, they were all up a dollar or more. (He also said he thought a woman couldn't trade but that, dear class, is a story for another day!)

As I became more and more subject to my own schooling as a trader, I became more what I now consider the literal victim of the "markets are only probability" teaching. It took a long time, and it wasn't really until my first glimpse at this study back in 2007 that I realized why not only me but many other traders I knew could at least sometimes read the language of the market almost as easily as they can read the printed word.

The lesson?

Intentionally resolve to evaluate the social/human context through which you analyze your data, projections, or probabilities. Do this first for yourself as a risk management tool, i.e., what are the emotional and social pressures playing on you, and second as a strategy tool for understanding market action.

The Risk Management Advantage in Social Markets

Andrew Lo, director of the Financial Engineering Lab at the Massachusetts Institute of Technology, has proposed the adaptive markets hypothesis. It is based on the idea that an ever-evolving ecosystem offers a superior model for markets. If you ask me, this idea makes complete sense given that biological humans would naturally produce biologically behaving markets. How could they do anything else? It would be the underpinning to my social markets hypothesis; as social creatures predict what other social creates will be doing, some will win and some will lose.

Bill looked over at Michael with a quizzical look. He mouthed, "But how?" Michael figured it was time to ask and raised his hand. "Denise, I sort of get what you are saying, but wouldn't it be a lot harder and even impossible to analyze the social underpinning of the market? I mean, how would you know who and what they are really thinking, and wouldn't there be so many variables?"

Michael, I am glad you asked. First, remember that all human brains basically work the same, at least at a fundamental level. We will get into this, but whatever emotional-social context any one of us exists in is actually the foundation for our beliefs and perceptions. (David Brooks, in fact, has just released a book on this very subject, *The Social Animal*, and I recommend it to all of you.) Knowing this makes it easier.

Let's start with a hypothetical ABC Fund that strategically includes human analytics and predictions in devising trading ideas and risk strategies. In the summer of 2008, no algorithm for massaging historical data could ever have foretold that if a major investment bank like Lehman Brothers went bankrupt, AIG would also be severely wounded. No historical precedent with the then-set of factors existed. Meteorologists, however, don't quit because they cannot say for sure where a hurricane will make landfall. Our ABC Fund looked at the drama of Bear Stearns' demise and the pervasive chatter regarding who else might fall most likely noted that the cries of moral hazard and the understandable potential limits of then-Treasury Secretary Henry Paulson's and Federal Reserve Chairman Ben Bernanke's appetite for bank rescues. (Which does by the way speak to the power of social context also, i.e., if we accept the social premise, then we can apply its inferences to "other" people.)

For ABC Fund, "A bank fails" would have topped the human scenarios list. So if you believed that the possibility of a bank failing could become very real, you could think what kind of trades could that produce. Our ABC Fund would have at least flat financials, particularly AIG, as a risk management strategy or maybe even more likely, short as a tactical bet.

Conversely, numbers alone, in an undervalued or mean reversion strategy, very well may have justified being long Lehman or AIG, given the extreme prices at which they were trading. Furthermore, if Andrew Ross Sorkin and his reporting in *Too Big To Fail* is to be believed, and I see no reason why it shouldn't, essentially *no one*, not even AIG, fully realized what would happen.

Of course, many a Black Swan believer will respond with the criticism that I can only see this because I know now about it. But I disagree. If we are smart enough to come up with the complex models we do, we are certainly smart enough to capitalize on skills we all have—people prediction—and start doing it better. In fact, I will go one step further and predict that for those who adopt this strategy, most of the swans in their view will remain white!

The Human Model of Markets

Think of an auction. Christie's or Sotheby's publish their expected (or hoped for) sales prices in terms of what prices are conveyed by—numbers. Auctions, however, frequently end up with the art changing hands for prices substantially different from what the experts anticipated.

What can we ever infer about the meaning of any particular price? In an auction, the last price influences the next price and stems from the antecedents of previous prices, but neither are ever a straight line. Someone bids out of expectation for reasons unknown to the crowd. A telephone bidder mysteriously bids even higher.

Bidders worldwide are competing to buy a valuable asset and likewise sellers are hoping to simultaneously sell their "treasure" to the higher bidder. So while trading isn't the same as auctioning off both the house and the contents from the most expensive house in town, it is akin to having

Internet access to all of the auctions all over the world at the same time. Diversifying means picking and choosing the best combination of what will work in your house.

So to get going down the right mental path, we need to think of the realities that all come into play in an auction. A bidder wants something and he or she wants it bad. So does another bidder. They bid beyond any previously stated "objective" assessment of the value. But, where did that, or any market value assessment, even come from? Ahh … what other people paid for it the last time!

Let's imagine that an auction for antique convertibles is being held in Palm Beach. One hundred cars sit on pedestals ready to be on the auction block. But this particular auction differs from the typical one squawking auctioneer in front and bidders with paddles in the audience. The auction house decided to try something a little different this time. Instead of one car at a time, they decided to auction all the cars at the same time. Each owner (or seller) will stand with an auctioneer and 100 auctions for individual cars will happen simultaneously. Ten thousand people have shown up (or are on the simulcast) to bid for these 100 convertibles So we have 100 cars, 100 sellers, and 10,000 potential buyers. (Some are just trading in simulation so they won't actually be buying but they may make a bid or two.)

As the bell rings, what happens? For one thing, it sounds chaotic. But is it? No, course not. Certain buyers came knowing they wanted to go home with three cars and they had a maximum of $100,000 to spend. Others came thinking that if they get a good deal, they'll buy one; and still others showed up thinking that they want that cherry red Mercedes at any cost! If all goes well, all 100 cars will sell above their expected price.

But what if all doesn't go well? Can you imagine how this scene would play out? What if someone shows up at the auction with a report from the local Better Business Bureau regarding a complaint about the official repair shop of the auction house? What if someone tells the person standing next to them that he has heard that some of the cars were in accidents but that fact has not been disclosed to the public? Will that guy bid? What about the other guy he told? Or, will that second guy go tell his wife who will run to stop her best single friend from over-bidding on the lily white 1973 Mercedes coupe? And if that happens, if she backs out suddenly, what will happen to the auction going on right next to that one?

Markets, Mercedes, or Monets

In market terms, let's take the alarming Flash Crash of May 6, 2010. Even without knowing the literal communication networks and bottlenecks, it gets a bit easier when you understand the fundamental auction model of markets.

Reportedly, one firm tried to sell 75,000 futures contracts valued at more than $4 billion. If truckloads of more antique convertibles started pulling into our Palm Beach auction, what would happen to the buyer's willingness to bid up the prices? In fact, would there be any buyers at all?

In the case of today's hyper-computerized market and the unfortunate reality, in my opinion, of so many venues where one can send their order, it is very easy to have a situation where at one simultaneous auction no one wants the goods. Word travels blindingly fast to the other auctions and, instantaneously, the value of that stock or piece of art or car plummets.

Furthermore, the no-bid situation defines essentially all market meltdowns. We call it a "liquidity crunch" but that simply means there are no buyers for those who want to sell. In 2008, the market, for what were known as structured financial products, actually had very few players overall. It had no central marketplace and the trades were done direct from buyer to seller with no middleman.

I realize that literally millions of questions, answers, and words in print have analyzed what happened. But at its core, once one of the main players let the cat out of the bag that they weren't bidding anymore, two things happened. Everyone else questioned whether they should be bidding. Think musical chairs where everyone sees that one chair is gone and someone isn't going to get a seat. Then as a courtesy of the way prices of assets are declared daily at the close of business, known as mark-to-market accounting, everyone had to mark down the value of similar assets (artwork or convertibles) on their books. As assets were marked down, none of the relatively small number of eligible players wanted to bid for more and that in turn drove the prices that could be agreed to for any sale even lower. It is an auction and when word spreads through the crowd that all the Monets (or Mercedes) are knock-offs of the real deal, the prices plummet!

As the saying goes, and as many a great thinker has pointed out over time, perception is indeed reality.

Chapter 7

Ambient, Circumstantial, and Contingent Reality

Stearnsmann Bank
New Hire Training
Day 2: Market, Risk, and Trading Psychology Lecture

August 4, 2011

Welcome back, class. I trust you had a few moments to think about our discussion last week. We ended with auctions, and today I want to talk about context and its criticality.

Did you know that how a human brain deals with even 2 plus 2 equals 4 depends on a preexisting condition? Wouldn't that given the machine and mechanistic conceptions of the brain that dominate so much of formal psychology thinking make you think that something as straightforward as elementary arithmetic would work the same in all human brains? As it turns out, exactly what happens within the structures of your brain when you think through or recount 2 plus 2 equals 4 depends on whom you were born to and at least what language they spoke. Native Chinese speakers, for instance, use different structures than native English speakers.

The implications of this for what we know about brain development are nothing less than revolutionary. It further underscores the now unlikely design of the "neural doctrine" and should call into question any report of the "this does that" type of brain research—even one that I am about to tell you about! Nevertheless, over the years, we were all taught the triune model of the brain—the higher thinking frontal cortices, the limbic emotional or lizard brains, and the ancient brainstem that keeps our hearts beating. While you will still hear that repeated, particularly in the world of finance, now you could consider the idea two generations behind. Supplanting it first was the idea that even a memory could be stored in bits across an entire brain; and now the growing research that says the area used for language and math in one language isn't the same as used for math in another. Who's to say that it isn't just language but that maybe being raised by an engineer versus an artist even influences which brain elements come into play in a given task. A model of mind development like this would actually fit an evolutionary paradigm better than the predetermined feature-function assumptions that remain standard to too many thought-centers.

But why does this matter to someone who makes their living making decisions about uncertainty? For one thing, just about everything is uncertain; but more importantly, what drives the end result of analyses, a decision to risk capital, if it is not the mechanistic procedural designs we thought were in control? To use the words of the contributors to *The Mind in Context*, our perceptions come from an "embodied-embedded" model that situates thought in the middle of a continuum that includes the physical body and its environment. This concept completely reverses the conventional wisdom still at work in standard market, risk, and trading psychology. The idea that a risk decision maker can operate like a machine becomes essentially laughable. His or her entire psyche exists only in a reciprocal and recursive relationship within a series of contexts and not as anything that looks like a sequence of computer code. Instead of finding that the more we reduce the brain to its parts, the more we understand, we are finding that the whole, at least for now, is greater than the sum of its parts.

Situational Specifics

Meaning arises out of the situation. Ironically, a German mathematician turned logician and philosopher, known as Gottlob Frege, deserves the original credits for noticing that essentially nothing means anything in isolation. History credits him with the "context principle" but even more ironically, at least to me, is that reportedly, he first articulated this in a book entitled, *The Foundations of Arithmetic*, which apparently was largely ignored by the intelligentsia of the day. He focused specifically on the subject of words, which while that might seem limiting, in fact, barely limits the concept at all given that we ultimately think in words.

In practicality, facts have no meaning without context. The intertwined circumstances in which events occur make literally all the difference in knowing what any one "something," even a market "fact," actually implies.

Think about it. Does any given market level, in any market (stocks, bonds, gold, oil) mean anything on its own? If you knew *nothing* else about the markets other than the Dow was trading at 10,000, would it mean anything to you? How would you know if that were a good thing or bad thing? Would you even know if it revealed bull- or bear-like behavior?

Suppose you make your living painting. You have spent your whole life drawing, coloring, visiting art supply stores, and dreaming of (or actually) strolling the streets of Paris. What are the odds that you would be able to come up with much of any meaning at all for any Dow level? Let's even suppose that of course you have seen CNN so you know that when you see the word Dow, it refers to something having to do with the US financial markets. But would you attach much significance to yet another trip through 10,000? Well, you might, if you understand that when the market goes up, the value of art goes up and when the market goes down ... well, there is always Starbucks.

We tend to overlook the fact that Dow 10,000, or even Dow 15,000, means nothing without knowledge and at least some modicum of understanding of what came before. In order to interpret, you need to know if the backstory emerges from a place at Dow 8,000 or 20,000. Take what is going on in the market today. We have had a downward slide into today, into August, but how do we judge whether it will it turn into a rout like 2007 or will it be like 2010 when we had a 20% correction only to come roaring back?

On the other hand, if you also know the history of market levels, you have the framework you need for 10,000 to mean something. Today, as we sit here in this classroom, we know that would be a very bearish number to hit. So at a minimum, you know whether that is higher or lower and, depending on your orientation, a long-only kind of trader or a perma-bear short-selling fund, you don't have to do much thinking to know whether you like or don't like the number and whether, at the moment, it means you are making or losing money.

If Context Means Everything, It Means Even More in Uncertainty

In 2005, Ming Hsu, who now heads the neuroeconomics lab at University of California, Berkeley, published (with his colleagues) a piece of pivotal research that looked into what the brain does when it comes face to face with a traditionally defined risky situation (where the probabilities are known) versus the ambiguous scenarios (where historical probabilities provide only a clue).

Classic decision theory assumes the brain handles both in the same way; but Hsu wasn't so sure and, indeed, they found differences in the route the blood takes through the brain, depending on the type of problem at hand. Hsu proffered the idea of an "uncertainty circuit" or the idea that a sort of red flag went up saying "more information needed."

Now this might sound innocuous or obvious enough, but if you take maybe the second most repeated rule of trading—"plan the trade and trade the plan," Dr. Hsu's research sheds a lot of light on why, no matter what anyone says, traders of all types find this so incredibly hard to do day in and day out, trade in and trade out. This supposed truism assumes a computer model of thinking. In practicality, it leaves very little room for context and certainly none for a warning flag that more information must be obtained.

Traders try to do exactly what they planned while their brain fights them to find more information or to scramble in the face of a clear, but maybe only subconsciously perceived, threat. I used to use the analogy of a jungle versus algebra, but now so many people have taken that statement and made it their own that I want to put it another way.

Your brain automatically and immediately understands the difference between counting out change at Starbucks and leading a football team, and you cannot fool it into thinking or reacting as if the latter is the former.

Whether you are a goalkeeper in European football or a quarterback in the NFL, you know your game plan only gives you a framework. If you see another player headed straight for you, you are going to make a split-second decision to get out of the way, get rid of, or protect the ball—no matter how many hours went into a plan "dictating" your actions.

Give it up—you can't force the uncertainty of an ever-evolving athletic contest into a formula that must be followed at all costs. Or, at least you can't, if you want to have any chance of winning the game!

Michael raised his hand. "Doesn't it seem as if traders generally don't appreciate how much their craft resembles sports? I mean, what you are saying is that the data only goes so far and then you have to put current factors together to make a judgment call, right? And really more importantly, if I am understanding this research, is that our brains are going to call up a judgment call play whether we like it or not, right?"

Yes, that is it exactly. In fact, shortly after the Hsu team's "uncertainty circuit" idea hit the academic streets, a group at Duke University led by Scott Huettel took a slightly different direction and showed that depending on whether you are flipping coins, working the equation $2y=6-4$, or deciding about buying GE stock, your brain will engage "distinct mechanisms." In the words of this study, "something special" occurs in the midst of ambiguous incoming information and that something is analysis of context!

For example, in a game of dice, you don't need very much context to know the odds of getting a 6 on any one roll of any one well-built die (six evenly sized square faces)—1 out of 6 right? You have all the information you need to make a pure probability bet. When faced with a market question, however, you have at minimum incomplete information and most often conflicting data that must be interpreted. Even worse, you aren't interpreting to solve for Y but to properly gauge the future perceptions of other market players who will buy when you want to sell or vice versa. How do you decide what they will likely think? Or more importantly, when they will think it?

According to Huettel, our brains go into what I like to think of as "jigsaw puzzle" mode. You look at the shapes and colors that seem to match and indeed you actually find them, even though they are simultaneously very different and very much alike. When these numerous possibilities present themselves, the brain mixes and matches until a given scenario seems to fit better than the next. It assembles a working context or set of set of perceived relevant factors from both what is known and what is predicted.

In uncertainty, we rumble through different possible pattern matches and choose which factors we believe and more or less how we rank each factor. These researchers say we actually mentally create fresh contexts built on the pieces and parts of prior knowledge.

So when you think about whether or not to sell AAPL, should you out-right exit at $400 because everyone who wants an iPad has one or should you move a stop-loss order to protect against giving money back? The "context-creator" goes to work to assemble what seems to you as the most plausible and likely scenario.

Unfortunately, markets, at least for the average trader, don't supply the immediate right/wrong feedback of a jigsaw puzzle, which often frustratingly leaves us stuck in never-ending wonderment over whether whatever decision about the "risk" we took, is, was, or will be the right one. We will get to the ever-present "fear of missing out" that comes into the contextual play here, but first I want to underscore the importance of these first glimpses into part of the brain's uncertainty processing.

The Duke team showed, at least in their experiments, that a critical node in the brain's scenario, the posterior inferior frontal sulcus (or pIFS for short) apparently thrives on uncertainty. It lights up with oxygen flowing through it like a Christmas tree when you flip the switch. It lies beneath the temples, and it strikes me as possibly a non-coincidence that many of us, when "thinking hard," feel compelled to massage our temples. Checking Google for "rub your temples" in fact yields pages and pages of how it helps headaches, serves as an acupressure point, and is used in yoga. Theoretically, you could extrapolate that the massage increases blood flow, as massage does, and in turn sends even more oxygen to the part of the brain which needs it most! More ironically, this pIFS evidently works faster than other nodes more associated with known probabilities.

Counterintuitively, we deal with uncertainty faster than we deal with arithmetic! Could this be because the vast majority of what we deal with is actually uncertain even though we typically forget that in reality we don't ever know what will happen tomorrow.

Whether we talk markets or life, instead of uncertainty being the exception, it is the rule. Known precision is the exception and, as such, it appears to take more time to hand off this relatively special circumstance to some odd part of the brain that deals in linear, serial, and exact questions. Maybe the broadcast of the glia cells simply works faster than the electrical network of the neurons—it seems conceptually at least plausible.

Beyond the neuroscience however the point remains: you gain psychological leverage when you make a set of contexts explicit with an intentional focus on the "meaning gap" between where numbers leave off and good judgment begins. In practical terms, resolve to know your contexts—all of them.

Chapter 8

Perception's Labyrinth

Stearnsmann Bank
New Hire Training
Day 3: Market, Risk, and Trading Psychology Lecture

August 11, 2011

Again, welcome back to this series. What a week we have had! Last week, we focused on context and, serendipitously, at least for our purposes, we have had a spectacular opportunity to watch firsthand the net market effect of decisions made under unusually uncertain circumstances. While we were talking last week, the Dow was falling over 500 points due to what became clear throughout the week was the interpretation of statements and actions of the European Central Bankers in relationship to whether they would buy Italian and Spanish debt. This social perception context was no sooner "understood" than Standard and Poor's gave us another one, the downgrade of US long-term debt. This in turn created a short-term vacuum in context, at least for Monday morning, as no one really has any memory of what happened the last time a downgrade occurred (reportedly by many pundits in 1917). The week has worn on with the market looking like a ping-pong game between plus and minus 400 Dow points, as market players worldwide try to predict what all of this means.

Today, however, I want to get back to the psychological structure of how we create a context in our minds through which we can organize a barrage of new circumstances as we have seen this past week.

Ambient and Situational or Contextual Building Blocks

Where do our contexts come from? This is the central question.

How much comes from the circumstances we see, hear, and touch, which begin outside our bodies; and how much comes from inside our heads, which are our memories, beliefs, and expectations? Some leading-edge theorists think almost all of our working mental contexts come from the outside, but this seems in reaction to much of recent psychological history being focused on the internal or egocentric.

It seems perfectly clear to me that *both* remain so critical to the end result—our perception of the right judgment calls to make. Just like the old nature versus nurture or genes versus environment argument, the debate now lacks relevance. After decades of arguing these questions, the generally accepted answer became "both." You would be hard-pressed to find a contemporary developmental biology scientist who doesn't think that nature and nurture *combine* to create who we become.

Hence, both external and internal contexts should be explored if one truly wants to commit to making better market mind game plays.

Again, let's say you have your stock in Apple. You want to sell it at an opportune moment and potentially buy it back on a dip. But where do you begin? Will AAPL again hit $400 for two trades within one minute of one day or will it trade through $400 on its way to $500 and then back again? The element of timing exacerbates the already relentless level of uncertainty presented to our minds by markets. The final whistle never blows.

Actually, that lack of a final whistle means that making market and money management decisions is for all practical purposes the most challenging decision front in the world. I used to say that obviously being in the military was harder than trading, but after a long conversation with a Special Forces agent, we agreed that military personnel, while under obviously the greater threat of loss of life or limb, actually at least have clearer decision paths. The timeframes—in the sense that you know when you are in enemy territory and when you are on base or you know when you are on leave and when you are returning—are generally known and the bottom line objective remains always the same—kill or be killed. The portfolio manager, on the other hand, can have completely unclear timeframes as well as objectives that keep changing, given that a market or asset price can reverse course and become friend, foe, or betrayer in an instant. The finality involved in war ironically provides a clarity that a trader or investor can never hope to achieve.

Beliefs (Here We Go Again)

This gives us part of the reason Markowitz nailed it when he ended his game-changing paper "Portfolio Selection" with the matter of "beliefs." Say you have an MBA or a financial engineering degree; you bring the intellectual context of quantitative analysis to two different sets of numbers, company cash flows or historical intermarket relationships. You were taught that analyzing one of these two groupings of numbers was the way to predict prices. You automatically go in one of two numerical directions.

1. Project expected cash flows for a fundamentalist.

2. Model the relative prices of tech stocks to say banks or big cap tech stocks to a certain type of economy.

So in reality you have an externally generated context—your social norm and what you were taught was correct *and* the belief it instilled in you as to the right way to analyze a situation.

This exemplifies the infinite loop of perception we spoke of last week when we contrasted the "essentialist" (separate entities) view of thinking. Where does the inner or outer context begin and end?

Beliefs, which implicitly include a feeling of confidence, influence (restrict) context; therefore, beliefs influence what we think we see or beliefs drive perception.

Beliefs and Feelings

Are beliefs cognitive based, or are they emotion based? Or, are they both?

Clearly beliefs have a thinking component. They happen in our head and if you focus you can literally feel the thought. We also can often find ourselves defending them with data. But can they be only thoughts, even in the old world of two or three separate mental systems? Is it possible to believe something that you simultaneously feel is *incorrect*? Of course not! If you believe something you also have confidence (a feeling of course) about it. Could it even be a belief without this associated feeling? Beliefs and the feeling of certainty are inextricably connected. Without that feeling of correctness, the belief would be a non-belief. By definition then, and in concert with the reciprocal system model of the body-brain-mind, a belief contains both thoughts and feelings.

Let's say we have a new problem to understand, analyze, or make a decision about. It could be anything but let's suppose, since it is our topic, that you want to develop a forecast for the price of a coffee futures contract. Or better yet, how can we make sense of the market moves this past week when they are unprecedented? Even 2008 didn't see the same number of sequential swings we have seen this past week. What would be the first step? Wouldn't it be deciding which information is relevant? And wouldn't deciding which information is relevant be greatly influenced by the beliefs you currently have about the best way to analyze market movements? If you are a CFA (or Chartered Financial Analyst), chances are you will turn to crop forecasts and demand curves. On the other hand, if you are a Certified Market Technician, wouldn't you first turn to pure charts of historical price action? And in fact, wouldn't you think that the other guy was going about it the wrong way?

Who could actually say which method surpasses the other one? Could anyone outside of academia really declare such a thing with a straight face? Those types of declarations signify that the person believed something, found the evidence to support it, and *then* made the statement.

Beliefs as Curator

Beliefs limit our range of view but they do it necessarily. Too many possibilities exist and beliefs curate how we go about looking at things. If we didn't have them, there would be too many seemingly new but not new decisions to make every single time we tried to think of something.

But here's the rub about beliefs that Camelia Kuhnen of Northwestern and Brian Knutson of Stanford showed in their paper, "The Influence of Affect on Beliefs, Preferences and Financial Decisions." Pictures of rotten food, erotic scenes, or plain old books sitting on chairs can change the feelings—or at least the context of feelings—we bring in either a positive or negative direction, and subsequently modify our beliefs and our confidence in a simulated stock/bond choice game. Rotten food makes you feel disgusted. Erotic scenes arouse you (or at least the graduate student volunteers in their study), and then the feelings induced through those pictures color how you perceive a subsequent decision.

And this is the key point—the context of feelings that gets created by an experience, even looking at pictures, modifies your perception of the next question you face. I also heard Heather Berlin of Mt. Sinai speak of a study wherein the participants were met with a graduate student overloaded with books. Said student bumped into the incoming participant, dropped the books and asked each one to hold the cup of coffee the graduate student had in their other hand while they picked up their books. The coffee could be hot or cold and the participants' judgments about the pictures they subsequently looked at turned out to be influenced by whether the coffee had been hot or cold!

Honestly, at this point, research has given us so many examples of how perceptions can be manipulated that we could be here all weekend, so just know that you will *think* you believe something to be less or more risky when, in fact, a professor may be able to manipulate that belief by showing you pictures or having you hold coffee cups and inducing a particular type of feeling.

In a particularly salient example for traders, the feeling of excitement from one situation (psychologically ambient environment) bled over into the level of confidence one brings to a choice and, in turn, changed the amount of risk it appeared prudent to take.

Seemingly intangible elements of context greatly influence what we *think* we see.

Perceiving—The Imperative Variable Essence of Consciousness

The percept, formally defined as being a "comprehension" or a "single unified awareness," means everything to our performance. Actually, if you think about it, perception means everything to everything. If we aren't perceiving things, we are unconscious, as in asleep or brain-injured or under anesthesia or, well … let's just say a bit worse off.

If we look at the mind game of markets as a game of playing perceptions—versus the probabilistic numbers game we thought we were up against—we will actually be better able to leverage the overly simplistic numbers and data we previously completely depended on. Clarifying perceptions over and over so that they match up with the ever-changing realities and eventualities of other players' percepts puts you in the real game. Easier said than done though, I understand. Understanding perception actually represents one of the oldest questions in psychology.

Traditionally, those who think about perception think about taking in sensory input (think burnt tongue, lip, or finger) and that sensory input alerting us to a "development." For example, in the visual realm, the way a squirrel completely blends into the bark of a tree when it is escaping my dog Ginger exemplifies a trick of nature in the predator/prey perception game.

Today, however, we have a boatload of new data to infuse into our understanding of perception. Foremost is new knowledge about the most basic of perceiving senses—vision. Typically we presume that we first see a thing and then we react to it. We have all been taught that our senses work essentially mechanically. Light hits the retina, reflects to the back of the eye, and so forth and so on. Well, it isn't quite that simple.

The article, "See It with Feeling," recounts the story of Michael Moy who lost most of his vision at age 3 and then at 40 had a successful corneal transplant, but at first could only see colors and shapes. As time passed, and presumably as he developed connections between the physics of his vision and the emotional processing tissues, he became "fluent in vision."

In fact, at least five studies on basic vision and affect or feeling show that in order for our eyes to actually see, they seemingly require emotional inputs.

Evidently, the visual cortex needs the context of emotional meaning to turn shapes, colors, etc. into anything identifiable.

So it appears that to be able to identify the fact that at this moment you are looking at letters, words, paragraphs—a book—your system for vision used the feelings it had long ago associated with letters, words, and paragraphs to even recognize that indeed a book rests in your hands right now.

A Linebacker Tumbles

A momentarily alarming example befell me recently. Ascending from the subway to Lexington Avenue, I "saw" a very, very large man beginning to tumble heels over head down the stairs. In microseconds, before what I could consider having any time to think, he had literally somersaulted his 300-plus pounds down about a dozen steps. In what seemed an instinctive move, I raised my relatively measly forearm in order to block his flailing size 14 foot from striking me smack in the face. Said foot did meet its resistance in the form of my sternum but seemingly miraculously I didn't fall backwards because I had also reflexively grabbed the railing to my right, which levered the resistance I presented. Of course, this incident took maybe three seconds, at the very most, from my upward glance to his landing place on the mid-stair platform (300-pound men being overcome with gravity works that way), but somehow my eyes instantly delivered the implications to my conscious brain.

> "OMG" that guy, who should be a Jets linebacker if he is not, is falling!!!
>
> He is about to (inadvertently) strike me.
>
> Ouch that hurt!
>
> Is he okay? (Yes, and two guys are helping him.)
>
> Am I hurt?
>
> Can I breathe?
>
> How did *that* happen?

This experience demonstrates the idea of seeing with feeling. In what has to be measured in microseconds, my mind assigned the value that he wasn't about to harm me on purpose but that I was in trouble if I didn't "prepare." Had I not both held my left forearm up and grabbed the railing with my right—the latter of which I had no conscious memory or experience of—I would have found myself falling backwards down quite a few stairs. If my correct perception hadn't been turned into action so imperceptibly (unconsciously) below my level of awareness, I would have undoubtedly suffered some major injuries. I might not be writing this today as most likely my head would have hit the concrete first. What saved me was my immediate reaction to the physical and emotional meaning and my brain's ability to process it without my even knowing it.

Trading Colors

Immediately, when I learned of the work on vision and meaning, it occurred to me that traders and portfolio managers of all types should reconsider what colors they use on their screens. The associations of green and red could easily be creating meaning and induce an impulsive move even before anyone had a chance to be consciously aware of it. Why not try, say, yellow and purple or black and white or gray? Or even change it up quarterly so as to dissipate automatic meaning?

And then I found a piece of research that proved it. Sure enough, "seeing red" isn't just a metaphor; it literally increases the speed and force at which we will move.

Do you realize the gravity of this finding about vision and emotion? You have been taught to ignore your emotions, yet you couldn't see if your visual cortex ignored them. Does that add up? Doesn't it once again underscore that fact that we have been working on the horrifyingly wrong assumptions about emotion?

More generally speaking, doesn't it dictate the need to intentionally include "emotion analytics" in a new strategy of contextual versus isolation or precision analysis?

Chapter 9

The Ironic Holy Grail of Risk

Stearnsmann Bank
New Hire Training
Day 4: Market, Risk, and Trading Psychology Lecture

August 18, 2011

Today is the last day of our four-week series and at least from the perspective of having object lessons to contemplate, our timing couldn't have been better. In the midst of some strikingly clear examples in the market's recent action, we've had a chance to discuss beliefs, context, and perception. Two weeks ago it was a rumor that the European Central Bank would not buy Italian and Spanish bonds that caused a 500 point sell-off. Last week, we went one way and then the other at dizzying speeds. Today, as we begin, the yields on the 10-year US Treasury note are hitting lows (1.9872%) not seen since the 1960s; while the ostensible reason for this is a rumor that a major European bank had to borrow US$500 million overnight. Reporters all over the planet have been talking about fear and panic while mutual fund managers try to tell everyone to be calm. This TV talk actually leads right into our subject for today.

Of course, most of the world still takes for granted the idea that our "thinking" brains reign superior over the dimensions of feeling and emotion. Eleven years into the 21st century, it remains axiomatic to assume the wisdom of controlling one's emotions. Whether we are talking markets or golf, the conventional wisdom preaches that logic and reason offer the obviously superior path. We assume, virtually without question, that logic and reason—and somehow by extension, mathematical calculations—represent the pinnacle of our power.

Yet, purely logically speaking, how can something that provides the fundamental, pivotal, and required element be inferior? It seems to me that, given the neuroscience regarding emotions required role, this prevailing assumption of emotion's inferiority ends up being the irrational part.

Glimpses that we don't fully buy it do exist. As the sluggish job growth drags on, CNBC repeatedly mentions bringing back Bob Shiller's "animal spirits" to the economy. In another arena, sportscasters across the globe never fail to highlight "momentum" changes, which if you think about it really refers to the collective emotions of the team and the crowd. Sure, the physical play or the score changes the odds, but momentum means emotion. After all, what happens to the mood when the leading team fumbles and the other team scores? Everyone, on both sides, instantly feels differently.

We even try to answer what has historically been this core issue through entertainment. In 1982, it was *Blade Runner* and its "replicants" who were trying to fake or even gain real emotion. Before (and after) that, the *Star Trek* series' central plot involved the never-ending competition between Captain Kirk's human judgments, which clearly includes his feelings, versus the logic of the half-breed Vulcan Spock. Vulcans theoretically had learned to control their emotions and were therefore supposedly capable of better judgments. Somehow however, even in fiction, everyone turned to the very human Captain Kirk to make the tough calls.

We seem to advocate one thing while simultaneously hinting that we suspect it isn't true. Is the human being inferior because of emotion or superior because of nuances in meaning that we recognize on a feeling level?

Why Control What Your Brain Depends On?

If a data source held valuable information, why would you want to limit your access to it? If information that you needed was there for the taking, why would you try to suppress it? If the same information served as a vital entity in your brain, wouldn't you want to know about it? If we *have to have* a feeling to see, to know, and to decide, how can controlling feelings be beneficial?

But yet the manta drones on: "control your emotions, control your emotions, and control your emotions …"

In and of itself, even the mantra lacks any real objective perception. Really now, can an emotion *alone* do anything? And I do mean *any* "thing"? Can an emotion enter an order to buy 5,000 SPYs? Can a feeling alone sell an entire portfolio at the low of the day, month, or even bear market cycle?

An emotion alone never lost a dime!

In order for anything to happen, one's physical body has to move even if it is only to type a few strokes on a keyboard. We used to need to call a broker who called the floor. So we used to have to exert more physical energy, in the form of picking up the phone and moving our jaw, than we generally do now. Regardless, our bodies have to move for something to happen. Bodies moving equate to action, and actions or taking action is the only thing that logically and literally needs to be controlled.

Somehow, somewhere, the thinkers of the ages failed to notice that feeling something and doing something truly are two separate psychological events. Yes, emotions do tend to have an urgency to them—they make us feel as if we want to act. But does wanting to act mean we have to act? Are they the same? Given that we can all learn to feel something without doing anything about it and given that we all learned many of those lessons just to get to adulthood, when exactly does the supposed re-merger of emotions and actions occur?

It doesn't matter what the feeling is (fear, frustration, hurt, anger, joy), all of them can be felt, examined, described, and understood without an action—or really without an "acting out" ever taking place.

While the role of emotions has been debated at least since the Ancient Greeks, we really do need to ask ourselves how we continue to mistakenly combine feeling and acting into one event? They are two and one—the emotion—doesn't automatically mean the second—an action.

A Coherent Theory Proposal for Behavioral Economics

Critics and proponents alike will say that the observations of our behavior gives us just that, a set of observations; but that behavioral economics or behavioral finance, the compendium of observations of our purported irrationality, lacks a coherent theory. And it does. For the same reasons we have been discussing—the dismissal of emotion in deference to the other psychological phenomena of thinking and acting.

If you have to have a feeling to make a decision, then all decisions have a feeling fueling them—it is as simple as that.

This acceptance of the idea of the essential context of emotion—the *eC*, if you will—offers a satisfying explanation for the perceived irrational behaviors listed in the compendium of the field of behavioral finance. Framing, priming, and antecedent events induce certain feelings and it is those feelings, now unconscious to most of us, that steer decisions and behavior. By systematically subjugating feelings and emotions to the other psychological categories of cognition and behavior, we miss their critical messages.

Damasio and his co-researchers were among the first recent thinkers to notice this when he wrote, "I now turn to emotion and feeling, central aspects of biological regulation, to suggest that they provide the bridge between rational and non-rational processes."

Right now, we don't stop to understand what we are feeling, so we simply end up unconsciously sending the energy of our feelings into actions. This process reduces the "static" or distraction of the feeling we experience on a physical level but if we learn to analyze instead, we find that that energy cannot only be tolerated but that it holds maps, clues, and directions. Understand the data source of the feeling—the real impetus—and you will not only understand the behavior but have a new and powerful lever into how to choose behavior that best serves your purposes. No amount of thinking harder, twice, or more rationally is going to change the imperative role of "emotions as data." One way or another, your cognitive unconscious will signal to your cognitive conscious through the conduit of feelings.

Sometimes the best ideas are the simplest—add feelings and emotions back into the conundrum about thinking and behavior and you have a coherent theory. All one needs to do is look at the context of the feelings, and the behavior will always be explicable. This doesn't mean you will like the behavior but at least you will understand it. It isn't that we are wired to be irrational; it is that we misunderstand and therefore misuse our so-called wiring.

In a world of research that is moving toward theories centered on multifactor emergence and contexts as the dominant new themes in psychological theorizing, putting emotional contexts in their proper place will pay off.

The *eC*—Emotional Context as the Missing Element in Risk Management

This unconscious acting out of emotional contexts creates risk in the classical sense.

Attempting to circumvent that risk, via numbers, again does not come even close to the source of the event—the feelings—that we believe we should be controlling but which our perception actually needs in order to operate. We may think we have deferred or eradicated them, when a moment to years later, we find ourselves acting exactly according to the feeling we tried to rid ourselves of. Just as Darwin suggested, this viewpoint transforms fear and anxiety into valuable early warning tools instead of discomforting nuisances or panics.

Think about children. We know what it means for them to "act out." We mean that they are crying or screaming because something feels bad. We understand that their behavior only reflects their feelings put into action. Why do they do it? Well, yes, they haven't learned not to—but what haven't they learned? They haven't learned other mechanisms to express or deal with their feelings. They don't have the power to enact any other strategy, as they don't know how to get on the bus by themselves (or calmly say "Mom, this isn't working right for me right now"), so they simply audibly, usually with decibels for amplification, "act out."

A very public, very painful adult example for all of us lies in the story of Hank Paulson and Ben Bernanke allowing Lehman Brothers bank to fail. In short, their fears of public outcry over government bailouts provided a context of feelings that prevented them from seeing how such a failure would reverberate. If both a social context of markets as well as an internal context of "emotions as data" had been the standard operating procedure, then the decision makers would have had a much higher chance of understanding their own motivations as well as seeing the potential consequences.

The *Wall Street Journal* reported, however, that FCIC Chairman Phil Angelides said emerging evidence shows government officials made a conscious policy decision not to rescue the investment bank. Apparently the then-Treasury Chief of Staff Jim Wilkinson (who would have worked directly for Paulson) wrote on September 8, 2008 that he couldn't "stomach us bailing out Lehman. Will be horrible in the press."

You don't have to be a shrink to realize that the phrase "couldn't stomach" means it will *feel* so bad that at least metaphorical upchucking, if not the real thing, would be in the cards.

Just then, Michael's phone vibrated, notifying him of a text. It was Renee asking how the trading psych lecture was going. They hadn't talked nearly as much as they had before he moved to New York, but calling her to let her know that Denise Shull was a speaker had seemed innocuous enough. He typed in: "Seems quite well." She is saying that there were what she calls feeling or emotional contexts that drove the '08 financial crisis." "Really, how well is that going over?" she immediately replied. "No one's head is nodding for one," typed Michael. "LOL, Great!" she texted just as Michael realized he really couldn't get away with—as much as he wanted to—typing under his desk.

Knowing, Not Controlling, Your Emotions (*fC* or *eC*) Can Be Your Secret Weapon

Could this be where portfolio managers and traders of all stripes have gone wrong? I submit to you in no uncertain terms that this misunderstanding of the role and usage of of feelings and emotions is indeed the source of market and money management blow-ups.

Everyone has not only discounted but overtly disdained a role for feelings. We consciously have attempted to throw out any knowledge or analysis of the most important factor driving our perceptions and decisions.

Linking together otherwise distinct arenas of cutting-edge research declares that the more uncertain a situation, the more our brains turn to context to make sense of what we are perceiving. Again, think of trying to find a place for a jigsaw puzzle piece. The more contextual puzzle-piece picking gets involved, the more influential one's beliefs, and feelings of confidence or fear, become. Feelings pre-stage perception and perception morphs into reality through the decisions resulting from it.

While of course humans can analyze numbers in ways that Yorkshire terriers or cucumbers evidently cannot, do we in fact even "do the math" in the absence of a feeling of confidence or even the feeling of desire to have some piece of insight or understanding? The feeling of belief in one's chosen mathematical approach, the natural desire to be correct, the parallel discomfort of discovering one made a mistake or circumstances have migrated so dramatically that work must be redone—all of these provide a highly relevant fC to what superficially looks like a logical, "rational" process. What we call cold data never exists in a vacuum.

The net message of the research into our behavior with investments proves beyond a shadow of a doubt that no matter how "smart" we may be, we repeatedly make the same perceptual mistakes. While believing in the supremacy of what we thought was intellect, we have been intentionally, although maybe inadvertently, circumventing our best clues. Thinking harder has not worked. It turns out that that this strategy may be like trying to nurture a successful garden by applying sun block to all of the plants, and then being mystified at the development of mutant vegetables!

We can't even identify the relevance of a number if the emotional processes in our brain fail to kick in. Leveraging this deconstruction of perception delivers not only a more cogent and useful explanation of how the 2008 crash happened but it sheds light on crisis after crisis that preceded it. In the future, it will provide a context into which a more comprehensive risk management paradigm can fit. It illuminates the new path we must take to protect ourselves and even profit from the next "dislocation." If one understands more of the process of perception, one can win a psychological war. If they don't, well … they get left essentially fighting on a flat Earth. Turning what seems ephemeral into data (internal data for managing risk and external data for seeing opportunities) presents a challenge that can indeed be met. Analyzing the elusive dimension of the non-quantitative while not necessarily easy at first can nevertheless be attacked in a systematic fashion.

Knowing your fC is the key.

Real Traders Got Me Here

I say this radical thing regarding the contexts of feelings and emotions with confidence because after years of lecturing, teaching, and coaching, I have simply had way too high a percentage of professional traders tell me something to the effect of "I am so glad I heard this! I thought it was just me! I've always suspected it, but everyone kept telling me to stay 100% in my 'head,' control my emotions, and not listen to my feelings. This makes so much more sense to me."

In fact, one gentleman at CME Group in March 2009, the day of the first big rally off the bottom of the 2008 swoon, came up after a talk called "The Brain on Risk" and said something very much like: "I have heard you before but I have one question. I get anxious and I don't hold onto my trades as long as I intend to. I try to talk myself out of being nervous but that generally never works. Almost every time, I get afraid of giving my profits back and so I stop myself out only to watch the stock go on a tear. What do you advise?"

I told him to "put the feelings into words and write out exactly how the doubt and fear felt." The conversation lasted a few more moments but nothing else of substance really transpired. Six months later, I got an email from the gentleman, saying that his profits had improved and he'd been handling his trade much better. And, in fact, I have heard variations on this hundreds of times now.

In fact, one could argue that Harry Markowitz had this rule in mind when he began thinking about the mathematics of a new way to construct portfolios. Returning to his stage one, bringing one's beliefs to the forefront and systematically uncovering the relevant *fC*, completes the objective he seemed to have had in mind. Knowing the feeling context you bring to any uncertainty decision effectively vaccinates you against ever being in the position of losing *all* of your capital.

The second way the primary derivative of *fC*, mark-to-market emotions, enhances your mind game occurs when you understand your own psychological position. As you become more and more adept and facile with your own decision dimensions, it becomes easier to understand to "read" the collective *fC* operating in the market via all or even a relevant subset of competing market participants.

The Initial Deposit in Mental Capital and Psychological Leverage

Well, we're just about done, gang, but if I can leave you with one thought, it would be this. As you begin to think about how to know, analyze, and capitalize on this *fC* or feelings context, think first in terms of managing risk by reducing unnecessary trades. As you become more and more comfortable with using an awareness of all that you are feeling—on a physical as well as emotional level—you will find that you make fewer poor decisions. In turn, there will be fewer times you need to recover from a bad day or drawdown. This alone will change your bottom line.

But it gets better than that. The more self-aware you become, the more easily you will be able to see waves of acting out occurring in the market. The fundamental job of trading the markets through "theory of mind" or understanding other people will naturally get easier.

We all know that the traders who make money year in and year out (and there are plenty of them out there) always work the game in this order anyway—manage risk first, seize opportunity second. It may sound a lot less sexy than shooting rounds of ammo into the enemy camp, but it keeps you alive and available to trade another day.

PART 3

DON'T BE A VULCAN

Chapter 10

Do We Ever Know What Tomorrow Brings?

New York, January 2012

Michael wasn't caught completely off-guard when he got to his desk on the Tuesday after New Year's only to find himself being called into a major interoffice meeting. The memo said "Regulations against Proprietary Trading by Banks." He had known this was a risk when he took the job but figured, like everyone else did, that the traders would end up somewhere. He knew enough now, even with only six short months on the "inside" to know that everyone would just start a hedge fund, join one, or move to Switzerland or Singapore where the US financial industry seemed to be headed anyway.

Sure enough, Stearnsmann Bank was phasing out all proprietary trading. His choices were (1) internally apply for a more traditional banking job (which sounded utterly boring) or (2) take the severance and run. Between round one 10 years earlier and being on the desk now, he was far too smitten with the markets to even consider for a moment going back to academia. He resolved that no amount of "Son, I told you soes" from Richard could lure him into a corporate container either.

As he experienced the heat of the action, he found himself more and more inclined to view and to win in the markets by leveraging the psychological side of decisions most of Wall Street overlooked. He could be patient. You didn't need to be in every move—you just needed to wait for your spots.

But what exactly would he do if he left? Wall Street teemed with people with more experience. Yes, it was true that lots of the exiled prop traders were indeed only setting up their own hedge funds and surely people would want relatively cheap guys like him to do the grunt work but that would take some time to pan out. Financially, he figured he could go a year before he had to have a paycheck. Between his 90 days severance and his inexplicable fortuitous luck in having found two Chicago grads to share a two-bedroom, rent-controlled sublet, things could be much worse—but still, laid off again? You have got to be kidding!

Dare he take a quick trip to see his brother Tom in Aspen? He didn't care what his father thought but he didn't want to come off as cavalier to a potential employer or, he had to admit, to Renee. He couldn't help but think, however, that airfares and lift tickets were cheap in January and he might even pick up a shift or two on lift duty. He had done it before and the Ski-Co probably still had him on file.

Acting more impulsively than was his norm, he began texting his brother, "Hey bud, have any room…."

Boston, January 2012

Renee had kept her eye out for an excuse to be in New York throughout the fall, but with the mountain of research she was studying it didn't sound remotely plausible that she'd be able to leave her lab. Plus, if she had learned one thing from her "crazy" mother, it was never to seem too eager or available when it came to men.

Unfortunately, on the day Renee's excuse finally arrived—an invite to a special public workshop by Denise Shull's group—Michael had left for Aspen.

Aspen, Colorado, January 9, 2012

As Michael lined up for the gondola on his first free day since he had arrived the previous Thursday, he realized how amazing one week could be. A week ago, he had gone to work at Stearnsmann early. He had expected to get a jump on the overnight action on the first trading day of the New Year. Now today, only a week later, his agenda for the day was to ski as much of Bell Mountain as possible.

It had taken only a moment for Tom to text back, "Come on out, bro!" He even had a perfunctory interview for the lift crew waiting upon his arrival. It was a tough job that required enduring every kind of customer and the worst weather, so it wasn't totally surprising that there was still an opening.

As he rode in the cabin alone (tourists aren't much for blizzard skiing), he wondered if he could lure Renee out of Boston. Her classes didn't begin until the end of January and to the extent he understood it, she was presently working on literature reviews of the emotion and decision neuroscience. She could read in Colorado as easily as she could in Boston, he figured.

Unfortunately, Renee declined. He didn't know she really wanted to come. She told Michael she just couldn't leave but that her father and some of his floor trading buds were coming to town. Apparently they took an annual guys-only trip over Martin Luther King weekend to Snowmass and would be staying in one of the legendary mountainside chalets. She was sure they would love to ski with him and maybe get a chance to see his almost Olympian brother in action.

He did appreciate that Renee's father, Christopher, could be a good connection to cultivate. In the back-back-back of his mind, Michael had been toying with the question of whether there was any way on Earth he could start some sort of trading operation of his own. He had some ideas about designing a strategy centered on the psychological aspects—beliefs and perceptions of other market players and beliefs and feelings of his own and his traders as part of the risk management story. He knew of the funds that were doing this with so-called scraping of Twitter, for example. Why not combine online communiqués with a purposeful, human interpretation of them? Plus, he knew his credentials in quantitative modeling and decision theory made for a respectable resume and everyone understood the government's role in moving trading out of banks so it shouldn't really look like he just up and quit.

"Maybe ... just maybe," Michael thought as he skate-skied his way down "Dipsy Doodle"—the Aspen equivalent of a bunny hill leading away from the gondola.

The Value of Experience

"Wow! These guys are good," thought Michael. Christopher and his friends pushed 20-plus years older than him, but he wasn't sure he could even keep up with yet another run down Hanging Valley. They had been up and down six times already, and it was only 1 o'clock.

On the lifts, they told story after story of their "good old days" in the 1980s—the boatloads of money that were made and lost, the wild parties, and the crazy investment schemes they all got involved in like penny stocks, fantastical tech ideas, and even Hollywood. At varying points, they had traded mainly options at the CBOE, some bonds at the Chicago Board of Trade, and Chris even belonged to the Merc. Evidently, the latter earned him the nickname "Merc Jerk," but it seemed affectionate.

Of course, his own father would be horrified if he knew where Michael was, but Michael couldn't find any reason to tell him.

It was obvious that Chris' crew sorely missed their game, even if they didn't fully admit it. Some were investors in start-ups and one funded a private prop firm (*Could he get hired?*), but clearly they all longed, at least to some extent, for the old days. When Michael asked them directly about what made them give it up, each in his own way said he realized at some point that the volume had "gone to the screen" and it was a different game to read the market through the screen.

One of them thought it couldn't be done at all and that the quants had total control of the market; but others disagreed and said they thought it could be done but they weren't willing to risk their accumulated nest eggs trying to be the old dog learning new tricks.

Michael made a mental note to ask more questions about how they thought it could be done on the screen. And at dinner that evening, he did.

"Guys, can I ask you a serious question?"

"Sure, Michael, have at it," said a guy named Steve.

"Well, today you said it wasn't impossible to make it on the screen—or at least some of you did—but you didn't really go into how. Would you mind giving a guy a clue? I mean, I know I traded on a bank desk, but, I mean, what if you don't have that kind of institutional capital and trading prowess around you?"

"Michael, you can't ever forget that you are only trading other people and their perceptions. Therefore, anything you look at must be viewed in terms of answering what are their future perceptions likely to be based on what is happening now. Now, of course, that is a tough question to answer, but there are some pieces of historical data you can use to help.

"The most useful one I know is 'volume at a price over time.' What that means is that you look at trading volume but from a different perspective. Most people look at it from the perspective of volume during a block of time, but that can only tell you so much. It shows you when blow-offs or extremes of moves most likely happen (the volume spikes when everyone on the wrong side of the trade gives in), but knowing the volume that accumulates at a particular price over time—something originally figured out by a guy named Peter Steidlmayer—can tell you the prices people really care or cared about. It tells you where action is likely to take place or what kind of action should happen when we get back to that price.

"I could go on, but hopefully that gives you an idea. It helps to see it on a chart," said Steve.

"I think I get it—but yes, I would love to see it on a chart. I don't think I have seen it before," said Michael. "I think conceptually though I see what you are saying—if you can see that many traders traded at a price, then you can extrapolate what they might do when it market comes back to that price."

"Exactly. And it is a pure way of seeing people through the chart—not a derivative like all of the indicators that people get so caught up with," said Chris.

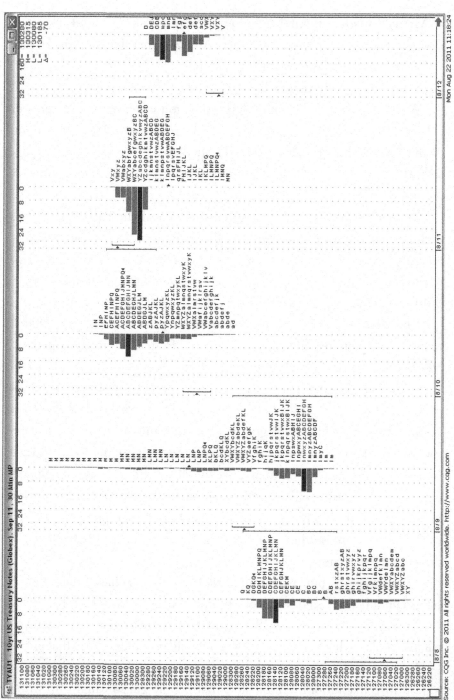

Figure 10.1.

Opportunity Strikes

"Son," said Chris to Michael, as they rode the gondola up to get in one last run together. "What do you plan to do once the season ends?"

Michael, a bit taken aback hesitated for a nanosecond for fear of sounding overly confident or out of his league. As his brain registered the thought of "what have I got to lose" he answered, "Well, sir, I know I am short on experience on a trading desk, but I have actually been wondering if there would be a way for me to start a fund or a trading operation of some sort."

"Really, well that's exactly what I was hoping to hear," said Chris. Michael couldn't believe his ears when he heard, "Would you consider coming back to Chicago?"

"Uh … well … frankly I haven't given the 'where' any thought at all. I've thought about strategy, infrastructure, and if I could raise any seed capital—or how to raise some seed capital. But honestly, that last one has had me a more than a little stumped. My dad wouldn't give it to me, my friends are academics, and well, as you know, my brother is a high-class ski bum."

"Perfect," said Chris to Michael's amazement. "The guys and I were talking while we were packing and we want to consider backing you if you are willing to work in Chicago and at least one of us has a management role in the operation. We figure between just us we could easily chip in a few million in capital plus the start-up costs for two years and see what happens. It would be a way to get back in the game without doing it full-time and you seem like you have the right blend of the art and science in your thinking about how to consistently make money.

"Honestly, we noticed it in your skiing—the blend of technique, your concerns about having the right equipment for the conditions, and your subsequent willingness to 'go for it' once you had the facts accounted for. We think lots of traders get too caught up in the idea of facts and never realize the artistic part, or the reading other people part and the knowing how to read oneself as the main events.

"You also seemed to intuitively understand what we talked about with Peter Steidlmayer's work. Understanding the implications of how volume develops over time goes a long way towards being able to read the electrons on the screen when you cannot see who you are trading against in the pits."

"Could this be happening?" thought Michael. "I'd move back to Chicago in a heartbeat for this chance!"

A Coup of a Different Kind

"If you are serious, I've got the perfect name for you," said Renee. "How about Coup d'État Capital? After all, your core idea is to make psychology front and center right? You want to take the latest in what we know about both people and markets—human perception, fundamental ambiguity, feeling contexts, and trading other people only, right? What could be a better metaphor for overthrowing the old rational and exclusively probabilistic regime?"

Michael loved it.

And in the interim three days since that gondola ride with her father, he felt a sort of fait accompli about at least trying the fund. He figured, "If not now, when?" With the capital and the expertise he was being offered, wouldn't he be a fool to turn it down?

Even though he was relatively inexperienced, and he knew it, he understood the value of having a plan while remaining flexible within the broad confines of that plan. The mistake too many people make, it seems, is either not having the plan in the first place or once they do, treating it as immutable law. Markets can have what these days is called multiple or dissociative personality disorder, and a trader has to be ready to recognize a new personality within a very short period of time. If nothing else, August and September of 2010 proved that in spades. Fortuitously, Denise Shull's company was currently advertising an advanced workshop open to the public. Maybe it was meant to be. Renee had received the invite by virtue of having been on the planning committee for her special lecture back at school and she, to his delight, had asked Michael to meet her in New York for the event.

Chapter 11

Mental Capital and Psychological Leverage

Advanced Workshop
Presented by The ReThink Group/TraderPsyches

February 22, 2012

Thanks, everyone, for attending our advanced workshop. As you know, this is a second-level course where we will extend the basic ideas about the brain on risk and begin to turn them into a real plan for psychological leverage. Here's the high-level outline of the four modules:

Review the basic concepts of the new psychology of risk and
    uncertainty
Mental and emotional or psychological capital
The spectrum of fears
The fractal psyche embedded in your market mind

The first will definitely be a review for most of you, but I feel it is important that we have a level-set to make sure that everyone is on the same page. Some of you have heard me speak at your MBA program, some of you have worked with me in workshops or coaching on your trading desks, and some of you came to me through a broker or an exchange like CME Group where I used to be a member. We will try to make the review quick, painless, and useful.

Key Concepts in the New Psychology of Uncertainty

First, let me itemize the basic tenets in our new theory of "your brain on 'risk'." Financial markets are human constructions and therefore they do not have some hidden law of physics buried in them.

- The task in any sort of investing or trading is to predict the future perception of other market players.
- Probabilities reflect past patterns and therefore do not include everything that can happen in the future.
- The numbers of markets are a language—symbols for meaning—they aren't absolute; and the real game is learning to read in this language.
- Judgment calls must be made to fill in the gap between where the numbers leave off and "alpha"—or exceptional performance—begins..
- The human brain relies on context to fill in the blanks when it is making a decision about something imprecise.
- Beliefs act as a preexisting condition, thereby creating implicit context.

- All decisions require emotion; therefore, emotion needs to be re-imagined as data in order for any decision maker to be fully leveraging their brain power.

- I categorize conscious or easily noticed feelings and emotions as follows:

  - The fC—or general physical feelings, which include tired, hungry, energized, nauseated, etc.

  - The eC—or emotional contexts, which connect ideas and experiences to judgments and decisions.

Psychological Capital

We tend to think our market asset is limited to our cash capital. We also tend to think only of our intellectual capacities as the avenue to an edge. In both cases, we omit a key factor in our success—our total mental or psychological capital. Think of "psych cap" as the sum total of your physical, mental, and emotional energy available to you at any one time. Like prices, it constantly varies.

Recognizing the reality and influence of psych cap offers anyone professionally involved with performance under uncertainty a whole new kind of edge.

Physical energy, for example, makes a difference. It seems very mundane, but human fuel—in the form that emerges from food, sleep, and exercise—matters. With athletes and performers, we tend to naturally appreciate the whole body-mind continuum. We expect them to tend to their bodies, their energy base, as job number 1; but we rarely, if ever, think of this angle as it relates to making decisions under uncertainty.

We again get caught in the idea that the job demands *only* our intellect. But let's say that even if it did, how can we optimize our intellect? Do you realize that the brain sits within the "energy field" of the body? Today's leading psychological researchers speak of "embodied cognition" and anyone playing the market should too.

For example, while we can't control the perceptions of the other market players, we can influence our likelihood of more correctly judging their perceptions. Beginning with physical energy and continuing on through mental and emotional energy puts you in a much better position to understand what the market (the other humans) is, or we should say are, really doing at any given moment. *For example, do not make any decision you don't have to when you lack physical energy. In other words, don't trade when you are tired—you will lose money.*

Research shows that sleep deprivation will alter your perception of how much risk you are taking in any given situation. Our intentions shift toward trying to find more profits while disregarding losses. It isn't that you will see it and take the risk; it is more like you won't even see it and truly miscalculate. In effect, your brain is firing on only part of its "cylinders" and taking risks just appear, or are perceived, as less risky than they are.

No telling how many times we have all said, "What was I thinking?", and that response may very well have been, "Why didn't I get enough sleep?"

It brings to mind former Treasury Secretary Hank Paulson as Andrew Ross Sorkin described him in *Too Big To Fail*. According to this book, Paulson as a Christian Scientist refused to take anything to help him sleep, even though the anxiety of the uncertainty and the potential ramifications of the decisions he needed to make had him lying wide awake at 3 AM. One of the enduring questions regarding the decision to let Lehman file bankruptcy is how no one saw the connection to the credit default swaps held by AIG. Undoubtedly everyone involved in the late summer of 2008 was working with less sleep than they would have liked. Could it be that the "gain" (no moral hazard) appeared more valuable than it was? And of course, the real risk just didn't even register?

The same advantage can be gained from the basic regime we all learned in grade school to eat at least three balanced meals and exercise. Keep your energy up! Thinking can be very draining. Studies have shown that even a simple cognitive task such as word generation can increase the residual products of energy processing by as much as 54%! Ever notice how tired trading can make you? You think, "All I am doing is sitting at the screen all day. Why do I feel like I've run a half-marathon?" Your brain uses energy, so of course you feel tired.

It pains me to say these things, it really does. I would truly rather be more profound. These points are so obvious, and yet so many of us don't take them seriously. We know we should eat better, get more exercise, and get to bed earlier, but we rationalize and let ourselves run on empty. We cannot win at one of the most competitive games in the world with a tank on half-full.

In fact, back in the 1990s, when I actually hired a psychological trading coach and she told me the same thing—over and over, I rolled my eyes behind her back. See, the thing was, I might have been a little tired, but not that tired. So, I didn't really notice it. I was healthy, in the best athletic shape of my life, in fact. Yet, was I really maximizing my decision-making energy? Oh yes, I worked out all right at what was then The LaSalle Club and Chicago's East Bank Club, often twice a day, as the firm I was at didn't want us trading during lunch. But sleep and food? Not a chance. I stayed up too late, I probably drank more wine than I needed on some school nights, and I didn't exactly face the markets every morning with that "I can conquer the world" energy that comes from tons of sleep, exercise, and a properly supported blood sugar level. I mean, really now, or that's what I thought. It actually seemed that I felt calmer with a little sleep deprivation. And as a single woman in Chicago, a little food deprivation didn't seem to hurt my social life either.

On the other hand, did lack of sleep and food help my trading? I seriously doubted it. I don't now and neither should you.

Market Athletes

Many trading managers want their traders at their desks all the time. It's like there is an underlying belief in a work ethic even though trading and investing are performance disciplines. Somehow they think fighting for every tick makes the most sense, yet this model almost always includes a regular cycle of "lose it and make it back" (but at least you looked busy!). Optimizing the trader's relationship to the market means embracing the multifaceted dimensions that can really only be called holistic. From the trader's point of view, the body and the mind always draw on internal and external context, so it follows that improving the physical dimension improves the mental, which improves one's market read, which improves results. Exercise can even make you smarter, or at least give you more neurons to work with, which has got to count for something.

If you have or can get control over your trading schedule, map it to your physical and emotional energy. Arrange your days so that you can be working from peak or near-peak energy the majority of the time. It might seem like you aren't working but, first of all, with today's technology, none of us has to be completely away from the markets. More importantly, it is better for our decision making success that we do get away from the stimulus (the market) to know what we really feel will happen.

Yes, I know, you feel like somehow if you step away, you will miss some great trade. Believe me, if one of you has told me that, a thousand of you have over the years. But tell me that you can't buy into fewer but better (and bigger) trades. The only people who suffer in that scenario work at the brokerages and the exchanges. They clearly already have revenue models that work just fine. You, on the other hand, want to maximize your own revenue model and the single best under-utilized way to do that is to accept the reality of the feeling and emotional energy context. Work to create your edge there.

Last year I convinced a trader at a big New York bank to do this. One day he knew that he just felt "out of it" and he decided that he was going to work on client stuff but not trade. The day turned out to be a "chop-fest," and most of his buddies on the desk and at his clients had gotten hurt. He saw everyone leaving and could tell they were wiped out. And then he realized that he felt great! (Okay, maybe there was some schaden-freude involved in that.) Nevertheless, he had managed directly to his psych capital and create what really can be thought of as psychological leverage for the next trading day.)

In fact, he got home and reviewed the day and knowing the old state-ment "non-volatility begets volatility" or "rotation leads to expansion," he knew that the odds of a breakout the next day were better than usual. He also knew that everyone else was licking their wounds and would be less able to trade well. I think you can guess the rest ... he literally had one of his best days of 2010. Why? Because he managed to his physical and men-tal energy and that gave him an edge—leverage via his psyche! If you ana-lyze the scenario, you can see he actually *added* to his edge by not debiting either his psych cap or cash capital accounts so that when he came in the next day, he felt energized and exceptionally clear headed. He knew where many of the other traders' heads were (cautious after a losing and frustrat-ing day), and he capitalized.

This isn't some one-off story. I have heard it hundreds of times. You can always create your own edge this way—no matter where you start from.

Net net—this means to re-characterize your job as much physically as intellectually. Write a new job description, like trading as an NFL quar-terback (or whatever your sport of choice might be).

Have the right type of game plan.

Know that good judgment on the fly will be ultimately what wins the game (remember your brain when faced with uncertainty *will* make judgment calls whether you ask it to or not).

Do everything you can to improve your judgment and execution in the midst of time and money pressure; this includes the very basics of sleep, food, and exercise.

Never forget, everyone wants to sack you! Don't give away an edge you can completely control.

The Psych Leverage Edge Versus Doing It the Old-Fashioned Way

For purposes of reiterating the importance of always thinking in terms of psychological capital, let's look at the issue from the opposite side of the fence—the lack of psychological capital and the "natural" debiting of it. Say you find yourself watching the markets and you begin to see a confluence of circumstances you recognize. Normally you would want to be in the action and you have heard all the admonitions that "you can't make money if you are not in the market." While things haven't quite matched up with the pattern you really want to see, you *certainly* don't want to miss anything, particularly if you have studied a repeated market event and worked hard on how to profit from it. So you move in and take the trade. Maybe you are a tad early, but…. What happens?

As you know as well as I do, it rarely if ever works out. Or it takes longer, right? Now what happens to *you* while the market does its dance? First, you get a little frustrated with yourself for jumping the gun. This equals psych cap debit 1—the distraction and creation of a new emotional context of frustration. Typically, not knowing what to do with that frustration, you get annoyed and in order to have a feeling of control you either exit or add to the position. Most of the time this is psych cap debit 2, because in both cases you recognize the impulsivity of the decision and feel guilty about being impatient. Guilt creates an even more debilitating emotional context, or as we have just said, a reduction in your psych cap or emotional energy.

We aren't very far into the trading day or week and you have some positions but they aren't quite what you wanted and, on top of that, you are annoyed (if not downright angry) with yourself. Typically, in the old "control your emotions" mode (let's call that CYE), your approach would be to rationalize everything you have done. You try to stay in your head.

Inside your head, however, your brain is trying to get your attention by sending you a signal through your feelings. Think about it. You *should* be annoyed or angry with yourself. You did the exact same thing you again said you would never do again! Now if you looked at the anger and said, "I see why I am irritated. I got in too early and I added or exited. Of course I feel this way," you would have a fighting chance at deciding the best thing to do next—wait, exit, or take a break. If you don't acknowledge that "notice" that your feelings are sending you, however, what happens?

Don't you typically act on them even once again? Or even if you don't act out here, doesn't the feeling context grow bigger, get louder? Then how do you feel?

Somewhere in this scenario, you undoubtedly experience a hit to your monetarily denominated capital. If you don't, consider it lucky.

Some traders play this out day-in and day-out. They try the "all intellect, all the time" approach to trading. They pay no attention to their physical or emotional energy or signals and they wonder why they keep making the same mistakes.

Creating Leverage With Psychological Capital

Take another psych cap scenario in which you leverage the asset properly. You are in a trade, you made a good decision and something happens to make the market turn on you. You get to the point where clearly you are wrong (i.e., the place where stop losses should be) and you get out. You lost money. It feels bad. You don't like it.

However, you decided to manage to your psych cap first and you know you have been debited. You know that, like an athlete, your playing apparatus has sustained an injury. Just like an athlete, you know that the quickest way to recovery winds through rest. So you actually leave the screen. (Yes, you can do it.)

What happens here to both your psych cap and your trading capital?

Sure, you took a small hit, but while you are away from the screen, you find it easy to remember that baseball batters hit only .300, if they are lucky. You work out some irritation by hitting the gym instead of the keyboard. Then what happens? Don't you get a surge of energy, and with it renewed confidence that your turn at bat will come again?

Compare the two—one where you manage *to* your mental and psych cap and one where you don't. Play the scenario out across three trades or additions to the position. In the plus psych cap, you have taken a hit, recovered, and come back ready to roll. In the negative psych cap, you have taken a much larger hit to your cash, feel like crap, and don't know what to do next. Let's say this happens 50 or 100 times a year. Multiply the effect on your P&L and your performance against the overall market or the coveted "alpha" and see which one is better.

Chapter 12

Mark-to-Market Emotions =
Risk Management

Advanced Workshop
Presented by The ReThink Group/TraderPsyches

February 23, 2012

To get started today, I want you to remember a few years ago when we were all buying the book *blink* in droves. Every hedge fund conference I went to was filled with people talking about it. Yet it seemed everyone secretly wondered how to "thin-slice" without simply being impulsive. I can talk about feelings and emotions as data but when you have to decide, how do you tell the difference between an impulsive one and one based on implicit learning or intuition?

Ironically, even when it comes to deconstructing a decision, the academics who spend all their time attempting to understand exactly how we do it, aren't even quite sure. We talk about expected utility and prospect theory, but to date, the world really lacks any broad agreement on how we actually make decisions. Of course, there are scores of books on the subject and, while I respect most of their efforts, just last year, the highly respected brain scientist Joseph LeDoux said we need a whole new theory of the brain when he appeared on the *Charlie Rose* show. We will discuss this later in the workshop, but recently David Brooks's *The Social Animal*, R. Douglas Fields's *The Other Brain*, the edited edition of a book called *Mind in Context*, and David Eagleman's *Incognito* have each made significant contributions, and in fact, offered completely new models of the mind—just as LeDoux has called for.

Today, at the risk of appearing highly immodest, I would also like to propose a unifying theory of behavioral economics that many say matches their actual experience. Simply add back feeling and emotions to their rightful place in the hierarchy of the mind. Doing so, if you don't mind me saying so, explains everything.

As I have already said, everyone's been mainly, if not exclusively, focused on only two of the three dimensions of our psyches: thinking and behavior. Even the new field of behavioral finance has mostly gotten caught in this web of an exclusively cognitive-behavioral paradigm. The idea of the triune brain, in which emotions are left over remnants of an early evolutionary stage, is now rejected by the cutting-edge of neuroscience, but many academic behavioral economists appear unaware of this development occurring on the other ends of their campuses. Proponents of this relatively new behavioral view of decision making critique the appearance of mistaken decision shortcuts (heuristics) and phenomena like over-reliance on the recent past. But if we can remodel the experimental models to include the all-important concept of context, particularly emotional context, everything looks different. In fact, all the questions start to be answered, and the right model begins to fall elegantly in place.

Lose the serial computer-based idea of the brain and mind. Instead think more in terms of baking cookies or thunderstorms, both of which have a finite set of ingredients or elements but virtually an infinite number of ways that they can be combined to create an end result. And the outcome always depends on the context—what came right before—to produce the end result. With cookies, it is the temperature of the oven. With thunderstorms, it is the exact way two air masses collide. Context is key.

In terms of your brain's development, it begins with a substrate of feeling and emotion. As infants, we know basically two broad categories of information, our mother as an object and how we feel. As children, we know a little bit more, but how we feel shapes how we learn language, math, and our self-concept.

The latest in memory research, for example, shows that the more emotionally charged an event, the stronger the memory trace. This appears to be one of the mechanisms by which events from early in life impact us later. We may not consciously remember them, but levels in the unconscious appear to act as sorting devices. The emotion of the memory works as a built-in context. When the brain needs to search for a proper context for new experiences, the emotional "tags" of anything similar in one's experience come into play. In fact, emotional meaning now appears to be crucial to the initial steps operating in our visual cortex or, in other words, in the mechanics of eyesight, one of the most well-understood parts of the brain.

So the bottom line is this: **The most predictive element of context is the feeling-emotional one, the fC or eC**.

To quote Jennifer Lerner of Harvard: "The empirical literature suggests that emotions influence numerous cognitive processes—selective attention, evaluative judgments, perceptions of risk and estimates of value, causality."

Therefore, take any decision you want to understand. Don't look first at the logic or seemingly lack thereof; look at the *eC* or emotional context. With a trade you can't understand, ask what was the emotional context? Stop thinking about your thinking and behavior; instead, understand the psychological environment. The emotions are your data—the data that, when properly analyzed, holds the best explanatory power!

Emotions as Data

How do you do a 180 and go from controlling your emotions to feelings and emotions as data? It may seem daunting but because you are going with the flow of your mind, it can turn out to be actually easier. Think of it as mark-to-market emotions. You spend almost all of your time monitoring price action, right? You pay attention to almost every tick. Why can't you do the same with internal data?

Expect to feel and then pay attention to your body and let it give you its message. Sure, there exists a whole variety of types of feelings and therefore different messages, but before you begin to decode the gamut, first you have to decide to listen to the messenger. Anticipate that you will indeed always be feeling something and make the effort to name what that is, even if it is the basics of tired and hungry, you will be moving in the right direction.

When it comes to emotional contexts, I realize that depending on how much pressure to suppress your feelings you have encountered, this may be harder than it is for the next person. We have been taught to use all sorts of mechanisms to circumvent the experience of emotion, such as intellectualizing, distraction, extra cocktails, and even exercise, to name a few. Some of us blatantly admit it: "Denise, it might be interesting and I might even benefit, but I don't really want to know—it scares me." Many feelings aren't at all pleasant, so oftentimes, it is easier to find a way around the discomfort. We may even have a walking knowledge of feelings while not having a clue of how we really feel.

Think of it this way, just like a feeling alone can't lose money, it can't actually hurt you. It may be very unpleasant or uncomfortable, but in and of itself can't do anything to you. You can feel emotions and literally just feel them. You won't implode or explode as many of us tend to imagine might happen.

Knowing oneself in the end is less work, more gratifying, and more productive than maintaining a labyrinth of defense mechanisms. You have the path of least resistance on your side. The benefits also definitely accrue over time. *Not* knowing yourself tends to create messes. The longer you live, the bigger the messes get, so the sooner you start, the better your life and your money management can become over time. You won't find yourself acting out things at 80 years old that you wished you would have resolved at 39!

So, once you begin to get some data on yourself, then you go into "emotion analytics" mode. Just like if you had any new data set to work with, first you would try to get the scope of it, look at it from different angles to get a sense of what you were dealing with, and then go about ways to monitor, track, and categorize.

Capturing Self-Data

In order to begin systematic emotion analytics, I have had a number of traders speak directly into an audio recording device and in turn find that instead of reporting on their various levels of fear, they are reiterating a CNBC-style market commentary. They are shocked that they never mentioned a feeling. On the other hand, I have had clients who attempted to begin to track their feelings and found themselves bowled over by how many different feelings they were having but prior to the exercise had no knowledge of. One of my early clients found that he neither liked a recorder nor a computer so he decided on one of these big notepads like I have here on the side of the room. After a few days, he had wallpapered his entire private office with large-print notes on the feelings he had as he monitored the market and his trades.

Begin to capture a record of what you are feeling. The simple act of acknowledging it, which by definition occurs when you are writing it down, will actually provide some protection from the destructive and unconscious acting out of feelings that you thought you were supposed to control.

Give Up the Getting Rid of Emotion

We will get to the part of what I and others are seeing as a new way to look at our emotional contexts through the idea of fractals, but for today see if you can feel the fear you have about having feelings at all. See if you can describe it. Just put the fear of feelings into words. That will be a great start! It should also give you the satisfaction and the feeling of a reduction in tension that occurs when you name the real feeling you are having. Something about finding your core, or part of it, simply makes you feel better than you did when you were trying to set aside a feeling or rationalize it with logic.

Plan to use these three steps:

Anticipate—the feelings will be there

Notice—resolve to become aware

Name—begin to name the different combinations of feelings

The first means just coming to terms with the fact that you have feelings and emotions. Once you expect to have feelings, the next task becomes to notice them when they occur. Think of this as the data capture phase and use the documenting we just discussed. On step three, the naming, let's start with the five basic categories of anger, fear, disgust, sadness, and pleasure.

We can also make it one step easier through understanding that while this "five basic" idea runs far and wide, Professors Tor Wager and Lisa Feldman did a summary analysis of all the fMRI scanning studies that involved emotion research and found an alternative view. They concluded that the "Big Five" may actually be higher-level constructions of what our bodies and minds are really experiencing. In fact, at that level, the role of external contexts, like culture or familial influences, can have a great influence on what we experience as fear, anger, or sadness. Wager and Barrett concluded with the suggestion for an idea of two basic dimensions of emotion — what I call "want more" and "want less." They would call it approach and avoidance, or if you think about it, academic terms that map nicely to greed and fear or the two ostensible emotions of the market and money managers. Additional researchers going back as far as 1980 also have submitted the idea of "automatacity" or an initial, pre-conscious, and automatic assessment if something is good or bad — a second two dimensional choice that would create the academic "approach" and "avoidance."

The Spectrum of Fears

To help you with step three, I want to give you the spectrum on which most of your conscious feelings are going to fall. Call it the FAD (or fear, anxiety, and doubt) spectrum. It has two primary ends punctuated with two extremes. On the far left, we have panic — of the kind seen in October 2008, March 2009, or August 2011. On the other end, we have FOMO (fear of missing out), or I guess what we should really call the panic of missing out as we saw way back in March 2000 with the high of the Nasdaq. You see it in short squeezes on a much more regular basis, a slow grind upward that some like to call "the melt-up," which ends with a very fast, high-volume long jump in prices. Between these two extremes of panic you have the more common spectrum of fear of losing or being wrong to fear of missing out.

Fear of Losing   Fear of Missing Out

←——————————————————————————→

Most of the time, you will find yourself between those two extremes. If you were to draw a nice version of this range and start keeping track with hash marks, you would find that you move back and forth through the spectrum. Fear of losing often turns to fear of missing out, which turns right back into the fear of losing, at least at the conscious level of awareness.

Michael leaned over to Renee and whispered, "Man, is that the truth!"
She nodded an understanding look back.

Fear Turned Frustration Turned Anger Turned Meltdown

While we continue to operate in CYE mode, what we fail to realize is that we arrive at what *seems* like a new and isolated decision with a very intact relationship with the previous decision. And unfortunately, that relationship has its issues. It can't help but be tainted with some quantity of feeling bad about oneself or frustrated with what the market "did" to us.

Every trader knows the scenario where one trade went bad and they sort of knew they shouldn't get into the next one but ... maybe, just maybe, they could get their money back and call it a day. "Maybe, just maybe" turns into a second, "Well, now, I simply have to get the money back and then I will quit," which of course never works and often escalates into a temper tantrum of trades. Then at the end of the day while staring at a gargantuan loss, they find themselves completely aghast at the damage they wrought. If I have heard, "I have no idea what came over me" once, I have literally heard it more than 1,000 times. The cloud of the feeling context from the previous trade deposits the frustration of wanting the money back, not just once but twice, three times, usually to the tune of half a dozen losing trades before the traders realize they have to quit (or the chief risk officer goes tap, tap, tap ...).

Take a look on the slide at this e-mail from a client where BIKB stands for "but I know better," or the kind of trade you feel exemplifies a rookie mistake.

I took a closer look at what happened that day and noticed two things. First, the BIKB trade didn't just come out of nowhere; it was preceded by a series of trades that I planned but didn't take (that would have won), and one winning trade that I exited early. I thought I was being cautious, but in fact my second-guessing of my planned trades was building up frustration and impatience. Without that, I don't think the BIKB trade would have had such a powerful impact on my psych cap. So the cost of those untaken or poorly executed trades was not just a reduced upside; they were "setting the stage" for a losing spiral.

BIKB trades set up feeling and emotional contexts (and also emerge from conscious and unconscious emotional contexts) of self-recrimination. Just catching yourself in those—and the feelings surrounding them—will impact your bottom line in a positive way. Knowing the feeling cluster radiating in your psychological environment gives you the chance to evaluate whether it signals a risk to be managed or an opportunity to take advantage of. Make knowing your emotional contexts one of your top risk management strategies. Make it even more important than your risk: reward money management ratio. I say this because if you put math to what we can call the temper tantrum series, you can see how your bottom line would look completely different if those trades are avoided. Extract even 50% of your meltdown episodes and look at the change your in your bottom-line. Plus, if you add back in the psychological capital you also will avoid losing, you can see how you will then be set up to take your next trade from a much stronger mental position.

The Best Moments for Invoking Discipline

It's true that the hardest thing to do—at the moment it needs done—is to walk away from the markets.

Vow to always ask: **How will I be feeling in the future if I take this trade?**

This is fighting fire with fire. Instead of telling yourself that you shouldn't take another trade, which is staying in your intellect, you are projecting yourself into your future feelings and using future expected "emotions as data" that helps you to *feel* the likely outcome which in turn gives you more power than using your intellect to lecture yourself.

Projecting how you will feel in the future works partially because it combats something the neuroeconomists called inter-temporal discounting, or the idea of a "a bird in the hand is worth two in the bush." Inter-temporal refers to the differences in time between points sooner and further away. We tend to value money we have right now more than future money. Inter-temporal discounting, in other words, is the academic term for jumping out of trades too soon. It relates strongly to the emotional context of fear of missing out. If you have profits, you want to grab them. The waiting gets very hard. You may give some back, and that too brings the virtually omnipresent fear of missing out (or fear of future regret) into play.

In other words, it it both true that time passing might very well make the trade worth less and that we feel afraid of it doing so, i.e., we discount the likelihood of the potential future value in our minds. We think "I don't want to give my gains back" or "I just take the money and run" but really we are working out of the emotional context of wanting desperately to avoid feeling regretful in the future.

A Special Case of the Personal Becoming the Market

We've all had fights and disagreements with those closest to us. It doesn't matter if it is a teenager, a spouse, or a girlfriend, everyone occasionally goes to work miffed over something. We could of course get into some tragic and funny stories here, but the bottom line is this: arguments make us feel as if we have no control. The other person just cannot see how ridiculous they are being and if only they would....

And then we sit down in front of a screen where we can easily push a button and our software programs will (most of the time) do exactly what we want. But really now, in those moments, do we really want a position or are we just trying to get control? How do we feel when we hit the button? We feel at least a tad of relief, don't we? We feel a bit better. We aren't so annoyed, are we? Unfortunately, it never makes the person we are angry with change their position. It rarely makes us anything but angrier as these trades … well, you tell me, how do they work out?

Michael just had to raise his hand at that one. "I have to admit this one. One day in 1999, my father, Richard, called me at Schoenberg with a commentary about how day traders were ruining the world. It was one of those days when the Dow was up 200 points and Internet stocks were bursting through level after level, and evidently Richard couldn't take it when he compared the stock price of his own company. So, despite the fact that he knew I was indeed at work day-trading at that very moment, he somehow couldn't resist the urge to call and voice his opinion. I got off quickly because I had the excuse that I wasn't even allowed to be on the phone past 2 PM, but 20 minutes later I found myself in eight positions that even I didn't really like."

Michael, that's a dead-on example. I could give ones from my own trading and many from my clients.

Fortunately as we learn more about emotions and decisions in the lab we can untangle what really happens and have a shot at mitigating the damage. Jennifer Lerner, whom we a spoke of a few minutes ago and who leads the Emotion and Decision Making Group at Harvard, researched the results of fear and anger on risk perception and found that anger tends to modify how we see a risk in a way that decreases our perception of it. As many of our clients have demonstrated, feeling angry makes potential trades look like a better bet than they usually are. And taking them doesn't give you the control you are looking for.

Need I say more?

Time to Take the Red Convertible for a Spin

On the other hand, we do have one more important dimension of the relatively conscious or consciously accessible (semiconscious) *fCs* that we must discuss. Like the frustration fireworks that light matches to our trading accounts, we will also all recognize this one.

Jimmy Buffett sings a song called, "It's a Rag Top Day." In his characteristic happy-go-lucky mode, he sings about the kind of days that one simply must jump in a red convertible with a sexy, smart companion and take a joyride. And well, I am sure Mr. Buffett didn't consult her, again, Jennifer Lerner also found that happiness decreases our recognition of risk. We all know this feeling. Things have gone well and it gives us a lot of confidence. It feels good and in the midst of that feeling, new choices or challenges look easier than they turn out to be.

In my mind, I kind of imagine our spectrum as having a diving board on the right-hand side, leading from the pool of fear into the pool of overconfidence. It happens when we have a good run, regardless if that run lasts for a few hours, days, weeks, months, or years. We feel like we "have it." We have finally acquired that mysterious ability to read the market that prior to now, no one could really deconstruct or intentionally create.

But again, I probably don't need to tell you what happens next, do I?

The bomb hits. In retrospect, we always know we got "overconfident," but we never seem to know it in time to prevent it. We give back lots of our hard earned "alpha" and sooner or later, land squarely back on the spectrum usually at the fear of losing or being wrong end.

A typical scenario might proceed like this:

- Beginning—fear of losing and/or being wrong at one level below conscious awareness
- A generalized doubt and anxiety about any market decision
- Time in the state above opens the window to fear of missing out but doubt lingers
- Fear turns to frustration over missing out
- Frustration turns to gaining a feeling of control via taking a trade
- Frustration being a close cousin of anger prevented us from seeing the risk

- Anger at ourselves for making an ill-advised decision ensues
- We want the money back and knew we were right to be afraid (Occasionally we digress into a "temper tantrum" of trades)
- Eventually we stop. We recognize we have to "reboot"

Then after the reset, we put together a string of good trades made mostly from the middle of the spectrum, until we end up at one or the other end of the spectrum—joyriding or moping.

Jump for Joy or Crawl Under the Covers

Can you see how the "environment" created by the last trade typically colors the next decision you have to make? While under the illusion of the whole CYE doctrine, everything we think we see and then everything we do emerges from the feelings and emotions that unconsciously spread from trade to trade to trade. We need to get to the levels of unconsciousness, or the fractal geometry in our perceptions. But let me leave you with one tidbit that interrupts or disconnects this context creep.

Feel what you feel—as much as you can feel it.

Get used to admitting to yourself (and if possible to someone you can trust) what you are feeling. Instead of trying to overcome or intellectualize a feeling (saying to yourself, "stop doing that"), say I feel like x, y, or z. Just let it be and don't judge it.

Simply put, the more conscious of it you are, and the sooner you get conscious of it, the more you can use this knowledge first as risk management and eventually as a tool for reading others in the marketplace. Whether they know it or not, they live on this spectrum too.

Don't be afraid to put it into words. In fact, reams of research out of the psychoanalytic traditions and now even decision science indicate that putting feelings into words, does indeed provide a great benefit. Putting feelings into words not only reduces anxiety but verbalization can actually allow us to work more effectively on a thinking level.

Here's another example from a client e-mail:

The first surprising thing I learned was about ambiguity: all it took to "embrace" it was to physically write down or say out loud "Yea, ambiguity!" I would laugh and then not worry about it; because the benefit of embracing ambiguity was not some great insight into what the market was going to do, rather it was an increase in energy.

You might be thinking that the great traders don't do this.

First, how do you know for sure? Second, I submit that at a minimum they are doing two related things, consciously or unconsciously. They are treating the markets as social contests and they have the emotion of confidence that they leverage. For the rest of the mere mortals who haven't developed this dual feeling-based edge, these steps we have talked about are how to go about getting it.

And last, for today, I want to mention a book called *Information and Emotion: The Emergent Affective Paradigm in Information Behavior Research and Theory*. I am advocating for an "emotions as data" regime change. In actuality, I am advocating for a conscious emotions-as-data regime change because I know your brain is using emotional meaning that way.

This book, however, is about dealing with information, the kind of factual data that market people normally look at, and its point is how to better present that information in emotional terms because the editors understand that information presented in emotional terms will be more easily learned and used. My point? If the information theorists are now dealing in emotion, shouldn't you be, too?

Chapter 13

Regret Theory—"Greed" Misleads

Advanced Workshop
Presented by The ReThink Group/TraderPsyches

February 24, 2012

The Left Edge—Fear of Losing

First, we all need to realize that it is in fact oftentimes reasonable to fear losing money. One would be nuts not to. We might be told we are supposed to get over it—have full confidence in fake precise probabilities. But what if we really did? What if we had no fear about losing or not accumulating money? We basically all need or want more money. How is it then that we are supposed to not be afraid of failure? It is simply ridiculous to ask traders to feel something else. In fact, given what neuroscience can show about the backdrop, sequence, and "automaticity" of emotion, the dictates about emotion ironically becomes irrational!

More importantly, as we were saying in yesterday's workshop, this fear (or anxiety and doubt), once you learn to use it properly, can be one of your greatest risk management tools. For example, it can be a very early signal of the need to exit—after you have learned to work with its amorphous, multifaceted, and ephemeral characteristics.

We will get to more of the "impulse versus intuition" question, but first we must re-characterize fear and its derivatives, anxiety and doubt. Embracing it as data (and even learning to assign it a relative value) can both be done and provides a significant trading edge, like psychological leverage. Once we learn to understand the relatively conscious fear of losing money, we can move to the more insidious levels where the fear of being wrong or even stupid resides. Those levels, which I call fractal-emotional contexts or F-eC, offer exorbitant amounts of psychological leverage in that acquiring an awareness of them can interrupt what seem like intractable acting-out scenarios that traders and risk-takers everywhere find so baffling.

The Middle of the Spectrum—Anxiety of Uncertainty

In between the extremes, you will be living with at least some modicum of anxiety and doubt just about all of the time. This is the curse of having an ongoing relationship to something as uncertain as the markets. If nothing else we all have some of the well-documented aversion to ambiguity. We want to make it certain because the fact that we don't know and we might lose or be wrong is indeed (and of course) nerve wracking. In order not to waste valuable mental and physical energy on averting the uncertainty of dealing with something that can't be certain, it pays to go through an exercise where you consciously embrace uncertainty, or really where you consciously embrace what you feel about it.

I conducted a workshop in 2010 where my students spent a weekend creatively working on feeling their anxiety about uncertainty. One trader, Ted, submitted what is now up on the screen. Take a look. I think you will enjoy his words.

I woke up this morning, still thinking about ambiguity and my natural aversion to ... well, mornings.

After a cup of Joe and a slice of shingle with a shimmy and a shake,
I set myself down to ponder:

Ambiguity

Coveted by politicians and poets … Disdained by science and law.

"political science" or "poetic justice"?

Artist, freed from the needs to record unambiguous reality.

Kodak moment or timeless Monet?

Sirens of synchronous and synchronized sounds.

Add feeling, and you have music.

And of the movement of minds and markets?

Rarely a consensus, always a conversation.

But with whom? I am not sure.

But for this ex-engineer to ponder its meaning, I can only say

The mind is a very strange place to be.

By the way, have you met my friends, Russell the rabbit, and his friend
Elias the cat

Figure 13.1.   Copyright Warren Photographic (www.warrenphotographic.co.uk).

Ted summed up our dilemma. He got a good laugh, that laugh of recognition. And, in fact, everyone who completed the assigned exercise found that they enjoyed reveling in their hatred for the ambiguity of markets. Most were surprised to find out how they really did detest dealing with constantly conflicting information. They intellectually thought that because they were market professionals, that they were "over it" or even in fact loved it. The exercise allowed them to put these unconscious feeling contexts into words and, in doing so, be much more conscious, and then more comfortable, with the anxiety the ambiguity produces.

By the way, a whole series of poems and stories can be found on the *Psychological Capital* blog and I encourage you to take a look. Many times, knowing what someone else feels helps us to know what we feel, or to get comfortable with it in cases where we don't like feeling that way.

The Practically Omnipotent Right Edge—Fear of Missing Out

Conventional wisdom about markets almost always refers to "fear and greed." Pundits and politicians alike think they know something when they reference these supposedly intractable emotions of the markets. Greed in particular gets inordinate amounts of play when it comes to assigning the blame for any kind of market, monetary, or behavioral fireworks.

Guess what, though? Greed might be considered one of the seven deadly sins, but in reality, the concept matters surprisingly little to what I am advocating as a more accurate and effective theory of the psychology of uncertainty.

Oh yes, it sounds good. It sort of satisfies everyone by feeling familiar and by making people feel superior as they channel their frustrations toward the faceless "evil" bankers of the big city.

Let me ask you a question. For how long has society been blaming both market meltdowns and trader travesties on greed? Has it been

25 years? 50? 100? 1,000? Niall Ferguson, in *The Ascent of Money*, traces the first instances of coins to approximately 600 BC, some of the first records of lending and loans to the 6th century BC, and hatred of the idea of interest to earlier than the year 1200. If he can fill a whole book with the cycles of affection and disgust for bankers and their ostensibly hip-attached greed, does anyone think that the modern version differs?

Yet have the accusations of greed truly mitigated any risk, systemic or individual?

I submit to you that it most certainly has not! We still find ourselves subjected to widespread market meltdowns and individual but influential cases of retrospectively inane risk taking. Take the insider trading trials we have been witnessing of late. Do we really think that $70 mil motivated a billionaire like Raj Rajaratnam to risk jail? Even on the other end of the trading spectrum, is it really the extra $250 that motivates the guy sitting at home in front of his market charts to risk his whole trading day, week, or month?

Ostensible greed presents us with a case where while it may look like greed and it may walk and talk like greed, it often isn't. Just like anger typically overlays a hurt, greed overlays what in the majority of time is the fear of missing out. Successfully navigating markets presents such a challenge that the idea of not grabbing every emerging opportunity just becomes too hard to resist. Indeed, after listening to thousands of active traders talk, I can verify that "flavors" of FOMO lie behind the largest percentage of trades or even whole asset classes gone bad. And management isn't immune from the feeling either.

Consider:

- Chuck Prince of Citigroup's famous line regarding the subprime CDO market: "As long as the music was playing, we had to dance."

- Less famous traders than Mr. Prince refusing to exit a position that is happily up 20–30–40% ("By god, it is going to the moon!") in a short period because they were looking for 45%, only to see the name deflate faster than a punctured balloon!

- The last people in a rally. Back in 1999, your parents' neighbor refused to buy an Internet stock because it was clearly nuts that all those companies were trading for hundreds of dollars when all they had was a vague plan, a catchy name, and warehouse office space in San Francisco or New York. But then, come sometime around the New Year in 2000, probably after a party where even the bartender was talking about the killing they were making in the markets, they thought, "What the hell, this thing just keeps going up, I must be wrong," and finally bought.

- The ever-present bane of the *human* high-frequency set—moving a stop-loss order to break even and getting taken out of a good trade moments before it races back in the desired direction. ("But I didn't want to give any back.")

This last iteration of FOMO probably derails more traders and their accounts than any other. It certainly plays into the frustration that debits psych cap and often turns into a spectacular incident of acting out a tantrum by making five or ten times the trades one normally would.

It works like this. A trader put together a respectable "social markets" entry. They "read" the current and likely future perception quite well. They have an idea of how far the trade could go. Because they have watched the market for many years, the idea ultimately turns out to be quite good. (Don't underestimate the power of unconscious pattern recognition.) In the meantime, the asset's price does what prices do—they make a move and retreat a bit, then they either reverse or keep going. It is in this moment of "rest," "catching its breath" that the trader gets hit with FOMO. In this case, it relates directly to giving back money they had. Believing they are being prudent and managing their risk, they move their stop-loss order to the point where they entered the trade. (Never mind that the social mind of the market doesn't know or care about that number.) And you know the rest.

Or take another common FOMO scenario. In fact, Deborah Tannen (the author famous for the 1990 book, *You Just Don't Understand*, about communication between men and women) observed that men truly detest feeling as if someone is getting the better of them. According to the book, they will go to what may seem like awkward or even absurd lengths to avoid being in what they perceive as the less powerful position. Little boys, in fact, will make outrageous statements (like on upping how far they can hit a baseball), even when everyone in the group knows that little Johnnie didn't hit it from New York to California!

Whatever the source of this feeling—chromosomes or hormones or training—I hear it all the time. Guys don't like other guys to get a trade they know about and didn't fully exploit. This is exactly what Chuck Prince meant when he said the music was still playing. Citigroup couldn't let Bear or Lehman or Goldman keep profiting from the creation and sales of CDOs and step back.

We'll come back to this specific feeling in a moment but first let's take a step back and discuss the overarching strategy for incorporating *f*Cs or feeling contexts into your decision making.

Anticipate Feeling Lousy—Regret Theory, the Logic of FOMO

Here's an irony for you. Did you ever realize that most of the time trading is going to make you feel bad? I can tell you that I have asked this question at probably a dozen seminars over the past five years and almost no one realizes it before we talked about it. Who expects to go to work, possibly lose money and, in fact, be set up to feel bad in almost all instances?

This is a direct consequence of the power and prevalence of the far right end of our fear spectrum. The fear turns to the frustration because with the rare exception of nailing the trade the outcomes fall into the following categories:

- Long (or short) and wrong
- Got out too early; left a lot on the table
- Got out too late; gave a lot back

In the end, see how traders are almost always choosing between the lesser of the evils, and then by definition feeling at least somewhat regretful becomes practically inescapable!

But we might be able to work with this if we step back and think about it, i.e., theorize. Theories are just that, theories. Logical ideas about how something may work guide research. Amazingly, a very potent one known as regret theory seems to have been overlooked in a number of ivory towers. Developed by two separate groups, the theory stated that if you add the desire to avoid future regret to a theory of subjective utility, or any one person's own view of what will serve them best, you could build a more accurate model of the way we make decisions.

Janet Landman explained the new regret model in 1993, but seemingly no one was really listening. She pointed out the patently obvious but mostly overlooked fact that many decisions create feelings of conflict. We want one outcome and sort of don't want another. But do we not want the second more than we don't want a third low probability but disastrous endpoint? Internal conflict in and of itself holds enormous sway over what we do. "Anticipated regret" maps essentially exactly to a money manager's experience of FOMO.

In verbal form, applied regret theory would sound something like this.

Choice A—get out now = take profits good; it might go further = regret

Choice B—wait for trade to move further = "let profits run"; it might reverse and I will give all my money back = regret

Choice C—put a trailing stop in = I get a chance to make more but I might regret giving it back when it reverts to my trailing stop (to the exact tick and then continues!)

In graphic form, it looks like this:

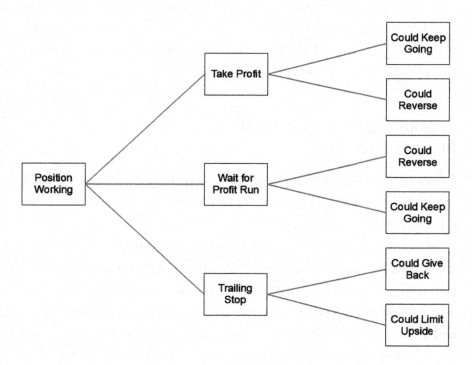

Figure 13.2

Traders get lost going round and round in this series of choices, without even knowing it.

Michael again turned to Renee and shook his head, "Yes!"

Isn't regret truly an awful feeling? I mean, fear doesn't feel good nor does anger, but that feeling that you made a mistake — sometimes a very serious one — and there isn't *anything* you can do about it…. You can't go back in time and get a mulligan. You are powerless to change the past and feeling powerless leads to feeling depressed. Is it no wonder that we try to avoid regret? Getting over regret seems to be harder than recovering from other feelings. It tends to nag at us…"if, only if." We will even dream about being in the alternative situation only to wake and have to relive the entrance into a "new" reality. Again.

Day-to-day trading exits may not invoke this kind of intensity but *entries*, or rather missing them, scare the crackers out of us. The market represents such an on-going mental challenge for us that watching our bus come and go without getting on blasts the fear of regret-o-meter.

Anticipating Regret Dilutes Its Inherent Strength

Understanding the inherent conflict in relentless uncertainty changes everything. Or rather, maybe I should say accepting it. Stop trying to make it certain. Stop trying to get rid of the conflict.

In fact, lean into it. Try to feel it. If you do, you won't act on it. Believe me I know, know, know that you want to know what to do — and the answer is simply feel. And watch what happens. I think you will be amazed.

If the context of feelings — the *f*C — reigns supreme in our perception and the majority of trades leave a residual feeling of dissatisfaction, what context do we bring to the next perception or decision? Always knowing the answer to this with the same level of perception and vigilance you normally apply to watching the assets you have money invested in will change your entire success rate with uncertainty decisions.

A Critical Note About Perfectionism

Every once in a while I run across a trader who for the most part just can't get into the market. In some cases they have traded or attempted to for very long periods of time. Yet most of the time, they watch the ticker go by and do nothing. We will get to this tomorrow in our lecture on the fractal geometry in our perceptions, but if you happen to be one of those people, you feel the opposite of FOMO. And while that fC will almost certainly always remain the most pervasive one, you yourself live on the other end of the spectrum. In your case, the fear of future regret revolves around how it will feel to have lost money or to be wrong. That is a stronger feeling for you than missing out.

It seems like an intractable problem, but in reality, it can be easy to fix. Once we get to the fractal psychology part of trading, in the next lecture, you will see. Just know for now that ultimately this default position tends to be easier to fix than an overly developed or sensitive need to "be in the game."

Chapter 14

Fractal Geometry in Your Market Mind

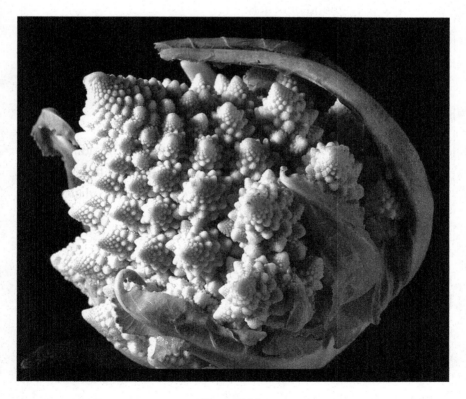

Figure 14.1.

Advanced Psychological Capital Workshop
Presented by The ReThink Group/TraderPsyches
The Penn Club, New York

February 24, 2012

What could Roman cauliflower have to do with the psychology of uncertainty? What if I told you the answer was, "Everything!"

What if I said, as important as all of the concepts in our new psychological theory are ...

- The background of beliefs
- The need for judgment calls
- Predicting human perception in an unknowable future
- Contextual influence
- The imperative fC and eC

... that the example of fractal patterns found in not only in cauliflower and broccoli but in human bronchia, tree branches, and throughout nature encompasses and therefore becomes even more important than each of the aforementioned realities?

Mandelbrot's Discovery of Fractals

Benoit Mandelbrot, a French mathematician who taught at Yale and worked in IBM's premier think tank, the Watson Research Center, discovered and codified the world of fractal geometry. Euclidean geometry deals in finite smooth lines and shapes like lines, triangles, and circles. Fractal geometry by contrast focuses on the rough and seemingly messy shapes of

nature, such as lightning, mountaintops, and coastlines, that often infinitely repeat. Prior to Mandelbrot's research, such shapes couldn't be accurately modeled by any mathematical formula.

Today, for example, the film industry sometimes uses Mandelbrot math
to create realistic-looking coastlines from a computer program versus film
shot from a helicopter or drawn from satellite photos. Even more to our
topic, fractal geometry makes sense of the data of price movement. It can
reproduce number series that appear virtually identical to the real price
series as reflected on market charts. As most of us know, prices are anything
but random. Early on, Mandelbrot noticed that clusters of large moves
occur within relatively brief periods of time.

For example, think back to August 2011, the week when the Dow closed
up or down by 400 points for four days in a row. That volatility occurred
after a rather sanguine and plodding pattern of price movement that had
lasted from March 2009.

The Key Idea in Fractal Thinking

A simple pattern repeated over and over forms the core idea of fractal
geometry. The pattern might be turned or twisted backwards upon itself,
but the original distinct element remains. Take our picture of the Roman
cauliflower. Can you see how the small nodes actually look like the one
big node or, conversely, how the whole head looks essentially the same as
each of the smaller nodules?

Likewise, at the very same time, while clearly the eye can see the virtually exact same pattern repeated in different sizes—a sort of natural
small, medium, and large—we can also see that each repetition fails to be
as 100% precise as if we had glued a handful of three-dimensional triangles
together. In other words, while clearly an elemental pattern repeats itself,
it does so in an obvious albeit rough way.

Mandelbrot noted this vaguely rough scaling, in either direction, as
the core property of shapes in nature. Think of the bronchia of our

lungs or the leaves of a fern. In each case, the whole can be broken down into smaller bits that look almost exactly like the larger entity. To use Mandelbrot's words, "the parts echo the whole."

Both simple fractals and multifractals exist in abundance in nature. It appears in fact that this design equation might in fact organize all of nature. Simple fractals scale in the same direction, while multifractals scale in different directions at different points (more like what you see when you look at a mountain range).

If we can now prove this principle across nature, why shouldn't it also apply to the architectures of our psyches?

My experience consulting with traders, as well as the work of a few highly respected and pioneering psychoanalysts, very strongly suggests that it does. And take this in light of the fact that even though I had studied classical as well as the relational, modern, and contemporary schools of psychoanalytic theory during and after my work at the University of Chicago, I began my performance coaching practice with absolutely *no* expectation of finding core ideas from psychoanalytic work so front and center in explaining to a client what was happening in their interpretation of their own and the market's behavior.

The Proof and Power of What Lies Deeper

In 2011, two books came out that speak to how or why knowledge of unconscious fractal perceptions in our psyches has yet to become commonplace. The first, David Brooks's *The Social Animal* notes John Barge of Yale commenting that while Galileo removed the Earth from the center of the universe, today's intellectual uprising displaces our conscious minds from the position of most importance in human behavior. He also paraphrases Daniel Patrick Moynihan as saying that the central evolutionary truth is that the unconscious matters most.

The second book, *Incognito*, by Professor David Eaglemen, came out a few months later. To use a direct quote, "The conscious mind is not at the center of the action in the brain; instead it is far out on a distant edge, hearing but whispers of the activity." He noted early on in the book that "Freud's intuition about the unconscious brain was spot-on."

Hence, I submit that not only does the unconscious matter most but within that idea, the easy-to-see fractal-like patterns in self-perception, expectations, event interpretation, and decision making offer a treasure-trove of data that can be mined to improve our perception and judgment calls.

Freud's Fractals

Freud originally articulated the well-accepted psychological phenomena known as "transference" and the "compulsion to repeat."

Transference simply means to move something from one place to another. In life, the concept refers to the fact that we apply what we learned about ourselves, our relationships to important people in our lives, and our perceived role in the world when we were young, to our perception of what is happening in our adult lives.

Fractals scale and, likewise, transferences scale. Each can be very precise but due to the complexity of human interaction and perception, rough at the same time. Like the patterns in broccoli and other plants, the repetitive patterns may not be 100% identical but they are so close that in practicality, they might as well be. Just the fact that anyone can see fractal patterns in ferns or human lungs obviates the need for an identical match.

When it comes to our psyches, eventually, if we peel back all the layers, sooner or later, the core fractal usually turns out to be our feelings about ourselves in relationship to our mothers. Think about it, they do give us our first feelings of self-worth or lack thereof. They are the first ones to respond or not respond to us. Many think the baby has no awareness or nothing that will stick with them when, in fact, the brain is developing based on the experiences it is having at the fastest rate it ever will.

When we first begin to look at our unconscious patterns, we probably shouldn't go directly to Mom. It's easier and more productive to pass through the layers of our history (and by definition our psyche's development) of our fathers, siblings, and other important people like coaches and teachers and events from our school years. We typically think that somewhere along the way, we discarded all of that and replaced it with a new set of "adult" lessons. In actuality, without working to become conscious of what simple fractal elements were built within our minds, we experience the present through the lens or prism of the past experience.

If you think about brain development, this is not so startling and of course makes sense. We build on the knowledge and experiences we have learned before, year after year after year, beginning logically at conception or shortly thereafter. This is a biological fact. Mother Nature meets the brain. Could it be any other way? The small pattern, the simple fractal, repeats itself because the memory traces laid down early on merge together to form the foundation of our temperaments, personalities, and character — or the multifractal design of human nature.

Over the years, I have called what I now know to be a fractal element in the development of the human adult psyche by many other names, such as:

- Echoes
- Emotional architectures
- Emotional templates

Echoes referred to the idea that we all have an internal echo, originally developed in childhood, of what our self-worth is. We hear the criticisms, spoken or unspoken, of our teachers, siblings, fathers, and mothers. And even if they didn't overtly criticize us, because children are narcissistic by nature (i.e., they think the world revolves around them), anything that happens that is bad (an argument, a divorce, an accident), they attribute to or blame themselves. Given the emotional import, the self-blame remains. The latter becomes an internally generated criticism and ends up influencing us in ways even more hurtful than an externally sourced one.

Initially, the characteristics of these special relationships interact with the substrates in our brain to create an emotional architecture, a style of being and reacting. Like architectures and templates, years later, our unconscious minds follow the rules of the architecture or template while often hearing the self-talk that remains as an echo of earlier explicit criticisms. Whatever I call it—echo, emotional template, emotional architecture—it operates according to the principles of fractal geometry—self-similar repetitive patterns or in the multifractal version Freud called the "compulsion to repeat." Add a series of transferences together, play them out over time, and you get a repetitive circumstance. In effect, you have the same natural phenomenon as a complex fractal built on taking elemental units and flipping them over, reversing their order, turning them right-side up, etc.

Frankly, I can't articulate the end result any better than Freud did. In his essay, "Beyond the Pleasure Principle," he said

[P]eople all of whose human relationships have the same outcome: such as the benefactor who is abandoned in anger after a time by each of his protégés, however much they may otherwise differ from one another, ... or the man whose friendships all end in betrayal by his friend; or the man who time after time in the course of his life raises someone else into a position of great private or public authority and then after a certain interval, himself upsets that authority and replaces him with a new one; or, again, the lover each of whose love affairs with a woman passes through the same phases and reaches the same conclusion.

LaPlanche and Pontalis, in their dictionary of psychoanalytic terms, defined the repetition compulsion that Freud originally discovered with words that might ring more true to a trader:

> [T]he compulsion to repeat is an ungovernable process originating in the unconscious. As a result of its action, the subject deliberately places himself in distressing situations, thereby repeating an old experience, but he does not recall this prototype; on the contrary, he has the strong impression that the situation is fully determined by the circumstances of the moment. These patterns acquired in childhood are forgotten and are instead acted out and repeated in life. It is reproduced not as a memory but as an action.

Bear with me here for a minute. Think about the definition of these relationships for a moment. Many of us recognize, for example, how our long-term partners often turn out to behave amazingly (and disappointingly) just like our parents. Also, it's not uncommon to catch ourselves speaking to our children in the exact same way our parents spoke to us—and being stunned to realize it. In the exceptional cases where people don't repeat the pattern, they often repeat the inverted fractal—or purposely take the opposite path. Still, even those opposite paths, while appearing different, wouldn't exist without the original pattern and are analogous to turning the geometric patterns upside down or backward.

And in fact, whether you know it or not, you each have a relationship with the market. It's kind of like a love-hate relationship. You have feelings about the market, you argue with it, you don't understand it sometimes, and you can feel controlled by it. Aren't those all the same feelings of a human relationship?

Simple and Multifractals in Our Market Lives

What happens when we make buy or sell decisions, or even when we are just perusing the market to make a decision, is that we experience a mosaic of feelings that we have felt many times before. We rarely, if ever, recognize it for what it is. We were never taught how the ingredients of our subjective experiences in adulthood were largely constructed very early on in life. Over and over circumstances recombine to falsely seem as if they are the "same old thing" inexplicably happening yet again but in reality, our expectations, interpretations and the all-important "*f*C" emerge and emanate from the past.

The fractals of our early feelings replay themselves out. If we really analyze the emotion, our market-to-market emotions, those feelings are very similar to when we didn't make the football team, lost a chess match, or listened to our father's complaint about us getting only a "B." The feelings induced in us back then, stick with us.

The market acts as the ultimate authority figure, and its tick-by-tick "declarations" tap into the feeling contexts from earlier in life. As adults, these contexts typically remain either unconscious or we feel they are "ungovernable."

The same, central, recursive nature of fractal geometry appears in our psyches as our worlds expand. Our mothers were intermittently available, so as adults we can find it hard to trust. Our fathers were highly critical, so we can be either highly critical of ourselves or become outwardly highly critical of others. The basic elements of perception we have formed about ourselves and others becomes infused into our expectations and explanations for circumstances in our ever-more complex lives. And in each of the aforementioned cases, we can easily substitue the human-group that is the market for the human.

The feeling we get while we are waiting for a losing position to turn around will map to a simple fractal of our basic expectation for ourselves.

Take a look at this example that I have posted on the overhead. The writer was a former big banker living on the Upper East Side of Manhattan and trading his own money. At first, he seemed in total control of his privileged life, then he confessed in an e-mail, "I have always felt I should have done better at things like school and sports." He said that to this day he could count on his mother's response to anything to be "not quite good enough"—an "A" should have been an "A+," a successful Wall Street career should have come with an even higher salary, even a birthday present of flowers should have been chocolate, or chocolate should have been wine.

Now look at what he said next. When I asked about what feelings he gets during trading, he made it easy to see both Mandelbrot and Freud in an e-mailed answer to a homework question about how he feels in the moments of his trades. "Almost immediately upon entering a trade (unless it moves in my direction right away), I feel it was a mistake and I have a strong impulse to exit before it blows up in my face."

Can you hear the fractal repetition of "should have done better"?

He even went on to unknowingly drive the point home by adding, "If it [the trade] goes my way, I am frantic it won't get to my initial target." Again, the original pattern of perception and expectation now has been transferred to his reaction to the market.

The context of feelings this trader brought to virtually every trade had moved from his mother's mind to his and then inserted itself into his perception of what the next market moments would bring.

Traders have a fundamentally fractal reactive pattern to what is a fundamentally fractal reality—the way prices move.

"Not Good Enough"

Life in general induces most of us to at least sometimes feel that part of the human condition that "isn't good enough." The markets in particular, with their tick-by-tick assault on our egos, frequently inspire this feeling. We don't like to talk about it in polite company (or even really admit it to ourselves) but, in fact, most of us on some level feels either not good enough or as if we are about to be not good enough. Once I heard a man worth hundreds of millions of dollars talk about a bad month in his business. I teased him about being worried, to which he responded, "It might all go down the drain." He laughed with that nervous kind of "maybe it is true" laugh. I realized I was hearing his fractal-emotional context of perception. He really did still feel like maybe he didn't deserve it or some other nuance related to being not good enough that clearly sprang from an earlier time in his life.

When we seem to sit passively watching the market's ticker tape, it can easily taunt you like some smattering of the people who populated your early life. Just about everyone has a father, mother, brother, teacher, or schoolyard friend who made them feel "not good enough." This stuff sticks with us.

Just because you decided on taking a long or short trading position, your "brain on uncertainty" doesn't change how it goes about making judgment calls in uncertain circumstances. The basic process steps through the context-belief -perception cycle because it can't help it. Uncertainty means— at least to part of your neural and white matter networks—that a black bear, ready to eat all your apples (and you with them) could be just around the corner. The more uncertainty, the more you can realize how much you are relying on contextual clues in order to make sense of the situation.

Shortly after I worked with the "not quite good enough" trader I described a few minutes ago, I talked about this story in a seminar I gave at the then Chicago Board of Trade. Within hours I received the following in an email:

> *I had been unable to pin down the issue that has been holding me back as a trader.... Bottom line is that when you mentioned the client who had always believed he should've done better in school, etc, it hit me like a ton of bricks.*
>
> *My issue has been somewhat the opposite ... that I always believed that I deserved more than I got, especially from my mother. It always seemed to be that the things I wanted were right in front of me, even to the point of being shown those things by my mother, but being told that those were things that other people were lucky to get, and that I should be happy with what I had.*

I thought I had come to terms with that in my life, but I see now that it has been affecting the one thing that means the most to me, trading ... I even acted out the emotion today in the market, I have been a stubborn trader, looking for that one or two more ticks, because I could see them there within reach ... only to be seemingly denied something I felt I deserved, for making a good entry, placing a good stop.... doing all the things a great trader should do, only to seemingly be denied by someone with more power than me.

This has been the one issue that remains in my trading that has held me back from super profitability, sometimes trading for three weeks with no losing intraday trades, and then giving it all back over a silly couple of ticks.

I believe these stories speak for themselves, but I am sure you can see the fractal repetitions of perception. Trader A could barely get a trade on before the fractal of his mother's feelings hit him. Trader B, however, could put on a trade, see it work, and be about to lock in profits before the transference or repetitive feelings took over. The first exemplifies a relatively simple fractal of mother's feelings infused into trader's brain.

The second seems to me more multifractal. It includes the second order repeating not only of the market playing the role of the mother but of the trader reacting and recreating the exact same experience—except he did it all for himself. He entered a trade, it became successful, he patiently waited for the end of the price action in his direction, but if the market did not provide what he thought it should, he reacted as if it were his mother holding back something she could indeed have given him. In doing so, he acted out his emotions toward his mother as a response to price action and ended up getting way less than he should have for a trade otherwise well executed. He became his own mother to himself in the same way that a triangle connected and overlaid in fractal geometry can become a star or a snowflake.

Neuroscience and the Unconscious Fractal Feeling Context

To put it in the words of another team of researchers, Tamietto and de Gelder, "There is now increasing evidence that non-consciously perceived emotional stimuli induce distinct neurophysiological changes and influence behavior towards the consciously perceived world." In other words, you may have no idea that you've been induced to feel this way or that but your body does. It signals inside your psyche and alters how you react. In the case of people dealing with market decisions, the induction occurs by the behavior of the price or the net effect on our profits and losses, but over and over, we deal with "non-consciously perceived emotional stimuli."

Michael instantly wanted to know "Denise, so let me get this straight. A fractal-like experience or reaction to the market or a trade could really be the re-enactment of someone's relationship with their father?"

Yes, it could, Michael. In fact, I have another example involving a trader's longtime relationship with their father. Ryan, an oil trader recently came to me with a funny situation. He had been trading well for quite some time when he realized he actually was trading without much of a real plan, so he thought he really should create and follow one. Almost as soon as he began trying to trade to his plan, his P&L took a nosedive. He couldn't actually follow the plan but he also stopped make money. He arrived at our conversation baffled.

All in all, it made no sense if you look at the situation through any of the annals of trading psychology wisdom. He only made money doing the one thing a trader is not supposed to do? How could that be?

To answer, we deciphered the meaning of the plan. When I inquired as to what his growing up years were like, he told me he spent a lot of time trying to "skate out" on his father. He proceeded to describe his rebellion of leaving home for good at 17, but by that point, he had a long-running saga of essentially doing the opposite of whatever his father wanted.

What is the simple fractal in this story? To deduce the answer, match up the roles and relationships in Ryan's basic story. You've got Ryan who is now a trader, his father, and the repeated rebellious or defiant acts perpetrated by Ryan in his younger years. Compare this to Ryan trading without a plan versus trading with one.

Who did the plan become a proxy for? Once Ryan had a plan, he effectively rebelled against it. The plan in effect became his father—without him having any conscious awareness whatsoever that a repetition or fractal pattern of behavior controlled the situation. In other words, an unconscious fractal emotional experience virtually pulled the strings behind the conscious scenes.

Furthermore, in the way that fractal geometry tends to be very clear and rough at the exact same time, Ryan also eventually discussed his tendency to fight market trends. Now, many people fight trends, and, of course, there is a series of relatively conscious feeling contexts that cause them to do it:

- Missed the trade and want to be in the market
- Fear of missing out on the move altogether, but can get the pullback
- The feeling that "it just can't go any further"

Since I have been consulting on Wall Street, I have yet to find someone who habitually fights trends that *doesn't* ultimately reveal a very clear and specific reason that arises out of their personal and family history. The easiest ones are traders who can notice that they want to prove they are smart. When we dig deeper, however, they always want to prove to someone (in my experience, usually their fathers) that they are indeed smarter than they were ever given credit for.

Resistance to Unconscious Feeling Contexts

It can be tough to see on one's own, and even if someone helps us, we have a tendency to resist these ideas. They make us feel too out of control of our own perception and experience. We have a very hard time accepting that simple fractals of perceptions and reactions got organized before we had any choice and now we are just playing our role. We like to think we have total free will and objectivity, and not that how we feel or explain something when we are 35 really stems from a smaller, less complex stalk of broccoli!

But really, the better question would be how could it not work that way? How do you suppose your brain develops? Does it just start working at say 5 years old? 10? 15? Of course not! Layers upon layers of perspective and knowledge develop most likely from even before birth but certainly from after. Most specifically, we gain a sense of who we are and how we fit in the world very early on. Childhood experiences pile up on top of ideas or states of feeling about ourselves that come from before we can speak.

All this time, the brain is "wiring by firing." We are learning ideas about who we are supposed to be, our place in the world, and what we can expect of others through our experiences. We don't just reset at 16 or 18 or 21 or 30 and throw all that out. All of the later experience builds on a very early foundation.

Of course we learn new things and we do mature and change; but if I have three stories to tell you about a key dynamic from childhood re-asserting itself into the process of dealing with the market, I have three hundred with the same type of obvious specificity.

Who would have thought? One of my big bank consulting clients once told me, "Denise, I understand why I should learn about my unconscious. I go to a therapist, after all. I just don't see how it applies to my trading. If you can make that connection, then I am all ears."

As I mentioned, I didn't even think it myself until 2004 after I had traded for a decade. Prior to then, I had left the so-called real world to study biopsychology because it seemed, at least to me, that the mind or mind-tricks our brains played on us obviously had to map back to the raw brain tissue. It appeared patently obvious to me that if we transferred and repeated in any way, then there had to be a prototype and template in the raw tissue. What I didn't expect to find was that the market and trades become anthropomorphized (or turn into people), and we "relate" to the collective of human behavior as if it were a real person standing before us.

Once I saw it in myself and in traders I coached, it was so obvious that I couldn't believe I hadn't thought of it before. My reply to the trader I mentioned a moment ago went something like this, "How could you stare at the unstoppable march of the markets as symbolized in the most implacable authority figure—price—and its projected inference regarding whether your current value is better or worse, and avoid having it tap directly into how you feel about yourself?"

Let me give you a few more examples. It really is the best way to grasp the reality of the influence of the fractal and unconscious emotional context we all bring along for the ride.

Trader C

A few weeks ago I gave a workshop in which two traders volunteered to share their trading challenges and basic life stories.

Trader C described himself as a very careful and deliberate thinker. He also described himself as not being able to leave the screen for fear of something happening that may require his attention. He usually planned to work out at lunch and let the mid-day doldrums pass, but repeatedly he found it very difficult.

Not surprisingly, he described his mother as very attentive and as one who had to have her finger on the pulse of whatever was happening at all times. He remembered one time when he was child she took a nap, and his younger sister, who was two at the time, wandered off to buy a candy bar. Of course you can imagine the impact his mother's reaction might have had on him (and the multifractal repetition that could be

analyzed there), but the bottom line lies in Trader C's context of conscious feelings ("I can't leave the screen because something that I must
attend to might happen") is a repetition of how his mother deals with
the world.

This feeling becomes the unconscious feeling context that modifies
Trader C's perceptions as he monitors the markets. As an adult, he believes
that is just a part of his personality and in fact it is.

What it is *not*, is intractable. Becoming conscious of what is unconscious gives us more freedom to perceive, judge, and decide in the
moment.

Trader D

Trader D could put together a very good run of trades. In fact, she could
do it over and over but inevitably ended her streaks with something I like
to call the BIKB ("but I know better trade"). For some period of time, she
would sail along in tune with the markets (reading other traders, of course),
feeling quite good, and really enjoying her trading, then—wham!—she
would do something stupid.

As she finished her story, I said, "Being a child in the house you grew
up in wasn't really all that much fun was it?" And she said that comment
hit her in the stomach, even after she had figured out some basic fractal
echoes of her childhood.

The BIKB trades could look life self-sabotage, but in reality, they were
more like water finding its least resistant path downhill. Having fun and
feeling good left her brain without a known context to work with, so it grav-
itates toward the one that is built.

So You Want to Build a Brain

I mentioned earlier that before realizing our psyches are fractal, I used a
number of analogies to explain the transference and repetition compul-

sions I could clearly see in virtually every trader I talked to. One of those analogies was an emotional architecture or the style of emotional activity in any given decision maker.

Digging a bit deeper, the analogy holds for the entire building process. Let's suppose you are a university and you are going to build on an open piece of land in New York like Governor's or Roosevelt Island. You might have a style in mind—the genes. You have limitations of the space—the environment those genes will be expressed in. Then you start building— you put in a foundation, self-awareness. You install the core of the electrical and plumbing systems—the social constraints/contexts of the world you find yourself in. You start building the first floor—the beginnings of intellectual knowledge. But what is that knowledge now shaped by? Everything that went before it, right? Furthermore, the foundation limits the footprint and the energy, and the water and waste systems define where unmovable columns and supports rise.

No matter what you ultimately do to the outside, or even how you build out each successive floor, these earlier elements "express themselves," even if you can't see them.

Eventually you can renovate or become aware of these limitations and modify the building. In the trader's case, this is the process of becoming conscious of how much the whole building emerges from the earliest decisions.

The Real Reason We Love Trading

Trading as a profession probably offers about the fastest way to reveal one's fractal emotional context. With the "transference object" being price movement, its finality and the rapid interaction a trader must make with it, everything becomes compressed in time and as a result, amplified.

Over the years, many of our clients have explained their love of the markets and their passion for the game. Some of them, however, can see that oftentimes, they have worked harder at learning to invest or trade than they have ever worked with anything. They wonder why they are so drawn to it.

One such person, who attends the original small group I still run on the first Monday of the month, said "Look, I signed up to make money. I signed up not to have employees or clients or vendors ... I most certainly did not sign up to have to figure out my baggage!! I mean, c'mon—who thought this trading thing was going to make me think about my relationship to my father?... But now it is clear that I must. Nothing besides trading would have made me see this—and I am glad for it!"

I didn't originally sign up for this either. I just wanted to teach Wall Street that the idea of CYE or controlling your emotions didn't fit with the latest understanding of the brain's need for emotion. I knew much about Freud's theories of transference and repetition, but I wasn't planning on going there with the original concept of "traders talking." But it happened. My early clients started talking and there it was, as clear as day—their basic childhood stories and feelings reoccurring in their reactions to the market and their positions.

Now I am certain that part of the irresistible seduction of markets is not the money but the tapping into an innate human urge, desire, or force to grow. It strikes at the core of competitive and adaptive instincts and serves up for the taking any unconscious psychological set-ups one has.

Your psyche doesn't actually care much about your account balance, it cares about your emotional capital because it is your most important asset regardless of whether you are in front of the screen or not.

Madoff and Rajaratnam's Probable Multifractal Acting Out

As in our earlier example, Ryan, who used his trading plan to substitute for a father to rebel against, one can step back and look at spectacular meltdowns and figure out a more than plausible idea of why certain traders did what they did. Take two who have been convicted of crimes related to the market, Bernie Madoff and Raj Rajaratnam.

If you analyze Madoff's behavior, it seems that what he wanted was to be liked. I actually met him twice. The first time, back in 1996, it stunned me when I went to his office to consider using his firm to clear my trading desk's trades. I didn't expect to talk to him but, in fact, he invited me into his office and we chatted for almost 40 minutes. At the time, I didn't understand payment for order flow. I would come to find out that it was perfectly legit, but it didn't seem so at the time. The second time I met him was at the Philoctetes Center in October 2007. The subject of the day's panel was the then-extreme volatility of the previous August and market structure. In my notes from that day, I wrote "he is hiding something." I don't say that for any other reason than to note his demeanor when I asked a market structure question. He shifted around in his chair and looked at the floor.

New York magazine recently published an interview with Madoff. It illustrates what I wrote for Reuter's *Hedgeworld* blog in December 2008 after having seen him in person. According to the *New York* article, he is very concerned about being perceived as a sociopath or as evil. He talks about being "upset with the whole idea of not being in the club. I was the little Jewish guy from Brooklyn." In other words, it appears to me that his whole cultivation of private clubs and exclusive access was probably concocted not just for marketing purposes but to satisfy his unconscious needs to be liked, to be a part of the club.

Likewise with Raj Rajratanam, the billionaire convicted on multiple counts of insider trading in 2011, though there is less data on him, the public pieces point to someone who very much needed to feel like an insider. Reading the news reports, he seemed to relish being at the center of the wheel, being the one with the power. The *Financial Times* reported that at his 50th birthday party, everyone wore T-shirts saying "Raj's Tribe." Also, he publicly stated that going to work felt like going to war.

I bring these two up because our defense mechanisms often make our own fractal elements and their multifractal consequences hard to see. It certainly can be easier to see it in others. It is worth trying to see because here is the reality of unconsciously believing, perceiving, and acting out of fractals—you almost always get *exactly* what you are trying to avoid.

PART 4

RUNNING MONEY WITH PSYCHOLOGICAL LEVERAGE

Chapter 15

The Rise of Coup d'État Capital

Monday Morning, May 14, 2012

"Here we go again," Michael thought as his father began his tirade.

"Son, can you tell me *why* you are obsessed with speculating in the markets? I mean, I truly don't understand it. With your education, you could be doing so much more. And what societal value do you provide? At least at Stearnsmann you played a role in hedging the bank against losses elsewhere in their business. Now you are just going to play with money for money's sake."

"What was I thinking even calling him on my way to my first day of work?" Michael wondered, as he pulled the ear bud out of his left ear. He willed his mouth to stay shut. It could only egg his father on, and with no response he would hopefully soon run out of his litany of criticisms.

You would think being estranged from one son would be enough. Michael's father seemed to push everyone out of his life. First, it was his brother and then his mother left him as soon as she got accepted to graduate school herself. Michael even now felt like cutting him off too, not only from this phone call but for good. He'd always made excuses for his father but he just couldn't take the nonstop berating. Getting to know Renee's father and his new firm's benefactors made him see that not every father felt compelled to itemize their children's perceived shortcomings. A part of him did feel sorry for his father as he didn't have anyone else. Richard's father had also been the same way so that is where he learned it. Grandfather Kelley thought nothing of continuing to criticize his son about decisions made almost 40 years ago. The litany was similar—why didn't Richard go to West Point instead of Columbia? Why did he go into business instead of serving his country?

As his father said, "Well, I can tell you aren't even listening so let's just end this call now." Michael realized that his father had no idea and never even bothered to ask if he was seeing anyone.

A Change of Scenery

It felt good to be back in Chicago. New York was okay but Chicago seemed so much more navigable. Michael had taken an apartment at Eugenie Terrace just north of North Avenue so that he could easily bike back and forth to their new offices in the original Chicago Board of Trade building. Even if his investor group hadn't insisted, Michael knew that he didn't actually need to be in the hotbed of capital raising or hedge fund networking. He just needed to get to work refining and then executing on his goals, objectives, market strategies, and trading tactics.

He and Chris had agreed that at least for now, they would cornerstone their strategy in directional betting across the most liquid futures markets. Chris knew these markets well, could lease his CME Group membership to the firm to save on transaction costs, and had a slate of recommendations for everything from charting to prime broker relationships.

Michael was particularly interested in developing his trading ideas around oil, gold, and the 10-year Treasury note. He had kept half an eye on oil and gold since the 2008 meltdown and he felt that both lent themselves to "social markets" approaches. As each were watched worldwide, he felt they matched up with a "numbers as language" philosophy and hypothesized that a psychologically based sentiment model would emerge slightly more easily than if he focused exclusively on any equity index.

Eventually he would take the Commodity Trading Advisor exam, but for now he needed to develop the tactics that would embody the strategies he and Chris had roughly mapped out. Besides day-to-day management, his potential ability to do this—bringing his previous momentum experience, his brief but valuable time on the Stearnsmann US fixed income desk, and his analytical skills—was what he was (at least currently) getting paid for.

He studied the oil boom from 2008, the gold explosion that more or less began in 2010, and of course the 2011 market gyrations. Each testified to how markets have personalities—they have rhythms and speeds at which they trade, at least for a while, and then they switch it up. CNBC and their contributors call this kind of thing "regime change," which is a metaphor for personality change if you think about it. The trick wasn't to get the very beginning of a move or the very end but the meat in the middle—and more importantly, to know (sense) the difference between when the price action was telegraphing a pending change and when no one really had a strong feeling and everyone is waiting around to see what everyone else is going to do—otherwise known as "chop n' slop."

He'd also already discussed with Chris about having a psychology coach on the team. He felt a little funny about it, but then he'd learned from a random guy he met on the lifts in Aspen that over the years firms like SAC Capital and Paul Tudor Jones had kept full-time psychologists, psychiatrists, or the like on staff. Renee, who technically was just an especially interested observer at this point, of course thought it was a good idea and told her father so. She was hoping to join the firm as soon as she could finish her coursework, but practically speaking, they all seemed to consider her a key advisor even now.

As it turned out, the request didn't faze Chris or the other partners at all. When they discussed it over a planning dinner at Gibson's, the overall reaction had been that it was a good risk management move. Michael didn't even need to answer any questions about who he might hire for the role.

Chapter 16

Quarterbacking
a Portfolio

Psychological Leverage
Coup d'État Capital In-house seminar
August 6, 2012

First of all, let me say thank you for hiring us. It's exciting to help get
a fund off on the right foot. Our first objective for this educational
workshop will be to help you lay out your own psychological capital
plans. We can of course tell you what to do and talk through it with
you, but, in the end, if it hasn't emerged from your own idea of the
material we can teach you, you won't believe in it and subsequently
will forget all about it when pressure strikes.

   Let's begin by thinking through how we normally approach a decision about uncertain markets, or to put it more correctly, when we
are making a determination about how people's perceptions will
change as events unfold, something that is fundamentally impossible
to know.

As professionals, we track the market moment to moment, day to day, and week to week. We track price movement in the markets we trade, as well as those we think are relevant, sometimes as close to 24/7 as possible. During our day shifts we sit in front of screens, watching every tick. We monitor the screens in order to keep constant track of anything unexpected or any development that might fit with some predetermined scenario we long ago deduced would likely lead to a certain type of market reaction from which we know how to extract some "points."

During our night shifts, we check the markets right before we go to sleep. We sometimes get up in the middle of the night to see the "open" in London and we usually look at our phones or CNBC before we even start making coffee in the morning. So we are tracking the numerical movements as much as humanly possible, correct?

And this on-going saga seems to be primarily intellectual. We track the news, make notes to remind ourselves of the upcoming economic events, and typically think of all of this as it appears: as a numbers game. I mean after all, as the numbers move they either create or destroy cash capital.

Would anyone disagree with the general description of how traders (and frankly other risk decision makers) spend their working days and even some holidays?

Yet, even though some people on Wall Street don't think anything of it, there are two underlying but imperative factors overlooked here. Tending to both can and will improve anyone's results.

Trading is actually a *physical* game.

Playing the "sport" of trading should be handled as if you are the quarterback of an American football team.

It is not purely a brain (or robotic arm of the brain) exercise!

The Physical Game of "Risk" Decisions: Body-Brain-Mind Reality

It takes lots of energy to have to watch something constantly. It takes even more energy to watch something that could at any moment bite you. Whether you feel it or not, this means you have a never-ending energy leak that, if consciously but uncommonly tended to, creates a psychological edge.

Most of you have been at one of my previous workshops, but this bears repeating, because for some reason everyone rationalizes this. In the case of playing this ultra-competitive game of markets, research shows that sleep deprivation makes you literally misperceive the risk. Your judgment will be off! You will see something as 2 when it is really 2.5. And believe me, you will go for the 2.5 or the 3 or the 4...the gains will seem easier to get and the risks not that big of a deal.

Given that 100% of the game relies on your good judgment, why wouldn't you create the advantage of being well rested? *Sleep is an edge.*

Along with that, most people don't recognize that thinking burns calories. If one really concentrates, the body and brain use an inordinate amount of energy. So at the risk of sounding like your grandmother, eating properly keeps your energy up and adds to that physical-psychological edge.

Last, on this basic level, we of course have exercise. We all know that exercise gives us energy and makes us feel more optimistic. Working off frustrations at the gym creates a physical boost, and that physical boost translates into a boost in attitude, which counts as psychological capital.

Simply put, the "machine" of judgment outperforms through the singular unit of the body-mind machine. Being in the position of "market decider" means you should re-imagine the entire endeavor as if you were the quarterback of a professional American football team. If you were, you would tend to your body first and foremost. Every trader who does so, creates an automatic edge over every one who doesn't.

At the end of the year, execution is what counts and it is psychological capital and mental leverage, built on a base of physical energy, that will make the difference.

It even applies to thinking of and testing quantitative models. Your brain works much better when sitting atop a well-fueled machine. Spend less time searching for some deeply hidden nugget of unknown market information, and instead get more sleep and exercise and invest in foods that make you feel good. The mind emerges from the brain and the brain receives its energy from the body, so the body counts essentially as much as your intellect. That is without even taking into account that feelings and emotions, your new core data set in uncertainty, communicate primarily through your body and not your brain. If the body is feeling the static of tired or drained, the feelings and emotions of risk-management and people reading can't properly communicate their data.

Game Plan Plays

If you are a professional quarterback, you go into the game knowing who is likely to sack you, where your receivers are going to be, and how you might need to instantaneously adjust on any given play. This is about reading the other team or reading other people, or the academic "theory of mind."

Playing the mind games of markets differs not a hoot! You've done the work on what to expect, but in the heat of the moment you need to always be anticipating and interpreting what needs to be done in terms of what the other guy is thinking or how the other less psychologically astute players will be handling whatever is thrown their way.

Intentionally interpreting through this lens of human context, or reading the numbers as the language, puts your mind into the true market (after all, never forget that you are only betting on whether someone else will pay a different price than you did). It means reading the speed and rhythm of price movements, just as a quarterback would the playing field. It means seeing developments on the periphery, such as the cash equities market is starting to rise, even though the futures are languishing in never-never land.

Everyone spends all their time searching for what everyone else doesn't know, when a lot more money can be made searching for what others are about to know.

Working the daily highs and lows and the commonly watched moving averages—these things actually tell you more than some obscure nugget simply because more people see them. Sure, every once in a while if you trade huge size in what is an illiquid market, the trade can get "crowded." We all know that in 2007–2008, the CDO (collateralized debt obligation) trade on the long side got *way* too crowded. That meant that just about everyone was long (and long by a boatload), and when one "trader" wanted to sell, everyone had decided they basically had enough. In order to sell, the only choice was to the put the asset on sale, hoping someone would want even more if it were priced at some fire sale price. Of course, once word got out that the assets might be "fake," no one wanted to touch them at any price.

Most of the time, however, you are all trading in big liquid markets with many players of opposing opinions. You don't want the opinion no one has unless you are prepared to wait and wait (and maybe wait some more) for them to catch up (which drains every type of capital we can name); you just want a little heads-up about the opinion they are about to develop. If you build on a base of energy and think in terms of what is the defense thinking or planning, you have just enough edge to exploit; and no matter what personality the market has, it can't be taken away from you. It is an information edge per se, just a whole different variety than the one "they" taught you to look for.

The Contexts—Feeling, Emotional, Social, and Fractal

Once you have the physical energy and the basic rules of the game down, you can move to leveraging the role of context. You should always know what came before, how that is perceived, and what the general explanation for it is.

Let me give you an example: on the Monday after Saddam Hussein was caught and on the Monday morning after Osama Bin Laden was killed, the average trader or investor expected the market to skyrocket. What happened in both cases? It started up but ended down, which reminds me of an old Chicago saying, "The amateurs trade the open and the pros trade the close." Amateurs want to run onto the field and start playing. Pros take their time, ensure their physical and mental preparation, and then wait until the opposite camp burns out.

But why is this true?

Think about it, if you have the information that conveys "the mood," the speed, and the rhythm of the day (or week or month or year) from which to judge, you can make a better decision about what you are trading against. Literally, your mind has more contextual details to make a judgment call about what the next play will be.

You are not going to find certainty, of course, no matter how many models or algorithms you run. The trick doesn't need certainty. It needs an increased level of comfort in the anxiety of not knowing. Now does that sound like an oxymoron? How do you have more comfort in more conscious anxiety?

It seems to work like this. Your mind tries to signal to you to pay attention; this is slippery ground and "I" (this is your brain speaking) want "you" (my "employee") to notice. If in turn you respond to that signal, of that feeling context that occurs in your body as much as your head, by acknowledging it, the signal seems to mark itself as "heard." Just saying, or preferably writing "this not knowing makes me … doubtful, anxious, fearful, flipping panicked …", you will find that the intensity lifts. Somehow your mind quiets a bit when we find and acknowledge its warning signals.

Kateri McRae's group researched what some cognitive neuroscientists call "bottom-up" or "top-down" emotion generation and found that when we use our intellects to try to override the "pay attention" signal, the signal just squawks louder. It might work to talk yourself out of bothering to be annoyed with your obnoxious brother-in-law at Thanksgiving (because he doesn't have any real bearing on your life or your P&L). On the other hand, for things that matter, like your bottom line, your psyche will talk to you; and it won't be with words you learned to read in school, it will be through the physical data of feeling and emotions.

Knowing Your *eC*

I know that most of your team here attended last winter's NYC workshop, but let's review for a moment. Before you get to the nearly omnipotent contexts of the *F-eC* (the unconscious fractal-emotional context), you can get lots of risk and market edge mileage out of knowing the *knowable* feeling contexts.

For example, where are you on the spectrum between fear of losing money and fear of missing out?

If you want psychological leverage, you need to elevate this introspective analysis to a priority even higher than knowing what the market is doing at any given moment.

If you don't know the feeling or emotional context you bring to any decision, market, trading, or otherwise, then you become the computer with GIGO (garbage in and garbage out).

Again, while counter-intuitive to what most of you have been taught, this endeavor implicitly provides you an information and judgment decision-making edge. It gives you the risk management tool that no computer can match.

So what if you miss a trade or two because you realize that the psychological context you were about to operate from would put you at a serious disadvantage? Think of the upside—you skip the trade as a risk management strategy, deal with the psych cap debit (with sleep, food, exercise, break, or talking through the feeling), and you come back energized and clear headed. What has happened to your capital? You clearly have saved cash and you are in the cat bird's seat ready to pounce on our new more accurate perception of what other players have been doing and what that means for what they are about to do.

A Very Basic, Very Powerful Psychological Leverage Plan

Let me boil the basic plan down to a cheat sheet:

1. Create physical energy.

2. Read other people.

3. Get the risk management edge through knowing yourself and how you feel (your emotional contexts) operating at any given moment.

4. Get the strategy edge by using that knowledge of yourself to understand others (their emotional contexts), which they most likely will act out (since they aren't doing #3).

5. Know when to push it because you have emotional capital and psychological leverage.

6. Know when *not* to push it because you are acting out of an emotional context fueled by the past, be it the immediate past or the distant fractal past.

Never Say "Dollars per Day" Again!

Many an ostensible expert will tell many an unsuspecting trader to try to make X amount per day and quit. A whole series of rules (like quit after three losers) also stems from the same outdated ideas about how the brain works. However, what are these supposedly unassailable rules for trading psychology really about? They are about your emotional capital. And you don't need these behavioral tricks to best manage your psychological capital. The truth is that you can manage your physical-mental-feeling state in the way an athlete or performer does.

You certainly don't want to try to make any given amount every day. You could do it for a week or so as long as you knew it was a training wheels exercise but, overall, the idea makes me crazy because it sets anyone who follows it up for failure.

It puts you completely out of sync with the varying rhythms and speeds of the market. It makes you put on the gas when nothing is going on and inevitably causes you to be outside somewhere when the market really moves. What you really want is to be out during times when no one seems to know what to do. Then you want to be able to recognize when a new wave is coming and get prepared to take advantage of it. Oftentimes, the market wanders back and forth through the same prices. Many a trader will get hurt during this time by feeling like they have to be in the market to make money or falling prey to the fear of missing out on a breakout. When the market is just wandering back and forth in a tight range, no matter what your timeframe, let the others who can't tolerate their unconscious fear of missing out take the first bullet. Then you be there to clean up when the market really moves. You will be creating the psychological leverage to be able to trade bigger and be putting yourself in the right place at the right time for when the momentum ensues.

Learning this strategy we are recommending—as opposed to a purely numbers based one—gives you something no other money manager or market can take away. Or, in other words, you will begin to have the confidence you will need to make the playoffs year after year!

Chapter 17

Decoding "What Was I Thinking?"

What's my Fractal?
Coup d'État Capital Monthly Workshop
September 10, 2012

This month let's return to the key idea of how we transfer expectations and perceptions we acquired in our history to decisions in the present. I understand that unraveling these unconscious fractal-emotional contexts can sound both impossible and may even be scary. If you said that you didn't want to know, you wouldn't be the first risk decision maker who didn't want to "go there". Of course, you can decide to skip delving in to it if you want, but I suggest you don't because it *will be* the feeling-emotional context that drives you when you most need it to *not* do so. Whatever *F-eC* exists in your unconscious, it will certainly make itself especially relevant when market moves become their most irascible.

Think back to 2008 or better yet, can you remember what it felt like—to you—in August 2011 when the Dow was swinging 500 or 600 points?

If you have worked with the patterns of chaotic emotions you feel in those circumstances and if you can then assign some of their intensity to your fractal set-up, you gain an edge over every competitor who cannot. Your awareness becomes psychological leverage.

Deducing Unconscious Mental Fractals

So where do you start?

First, we must figure out the architecture of your general reactionary style. I don't mean that we simply want to know how you tend to react, but rather that we want the unconscious reasons for your tendencies and the raw data of what goes through your mind when you are challenged with the uncertainty.

Here's an exercise, loosely adapted from Harville Hendrix's book, *Getting the Love You Want,* that I would like each of you to commit to doing. It will put you on the path to being able to recognize your fractal, repetitive psychological set-ups.

Step 1

Find a voice recorder and record your stream of consciousness through the sequence of two to three trades or decisions. Perhaps some of you take 15 minutes to execute three trades and some of you take 15 days. For those of you who take 15 days or even 15 months, no, you don't have to record every single thing you think the entire time! Put the recorder on as you are thinking about getting in or out of a position and start talking.

We don't need a narration of the market action even though that will be your temptation. We want the self-talk or the stream of consciousness that relates to your observations of yourself. If you can't "hear" it, try it from the point of view of one or both of your parents. Imagine they were in the room commenting on your decision making. Work on this over a couple of weeks and then set the recordings aside.

Step 2

Next, answer this series of questions in this order.

Write down five to 10 memories from before you were 18 years old. They can be anything that comes to mind — sports, school, friends, teachers, or holidays. Look at pictures or yearbooks or ask your family if you can't remember much.

- From that list, pick three that stand out from the rest. Maybe they still have an emotional charge, maybe you even think of them every once in a while. Myself for example — as seniors in high school my nemesis Jane looked at me one day and said *"Oh, you should be a gym teacher."* Well now she was valedictorian, teacher's pet, and if nothing else, I will give her smart— but for some reason she wanted me to feel not smart enough to handle anything outside of gym! I still remember it and I know it hasn't lost all of its sting because one, I even remember it and two, thinking about letting her know I did well in graduate school has a certain appeal. Memories like that are the kinds that will be most useful for this exercise.

For these three memories, write the story of what happened. It doesn't have to be *War and Peace*, just a kind of news report on who, what, where, why, and when, more or less as I just did.

Next, take these stories and look at them from a different point of view. Ask what the *other* people in the story were feeling or what it seemed like they were feeling. In my case, my good friends were sitting around and they burst out laughing; fortunately not at me but at Jane for her misjudgment and clear put-down (nothing against gym teachers; actually, it sounds like a very fun job now that I think about it!).

Last, write down how the situation made you feel in the moment and what you told yourself about the situation.

Once you get this far, set the writing and the recordings aside for a few days or weeks. Just let both steps simmer in the back of your mind. (Listen to yourself here. Work at the pace that feels right to you.)

Step 3

Next, while you let the first two steps "marinate," consider, if it feels comfortable, making some sort of record of your dreams.

In this case, what actually happens doesn't matter one iota. What matters is the sequence of feelings and emotions in the dream; or, in other words, those feelings that you wake up with in reaction to the events in the dream.

I know it isn't necessarily easy to remember but do what you can. Keep a bedside notebook or your phone nearby so you can jot down your thoughts and feelings right away. For the purposes of this exercise, try to get three to four, but also know that this is a good habit to get into because the emotional sequences in dreams usually escape the filters of waking life.

Step 4

For this step, summarize the following from the data of your memories and if you worked at all with your dreams, supplement your answer with that emotional data.

- What do I expect for myself?
- How do I expect things to turn out?
- How do I seem to feel about myself?
- What kind of labels do I talk about myself with?
- What fears come up?
- How do I react to others?
- How do I react to being told something other than what I want to hear?

You are trying to arrive at the basic story of your typically unconscious feelings. Just do the best you can with whatever your mind serves up.

Step 5

Go back to your trading recordings and summarize what feelings came up during your decision-making moments. Again, we're looking for the themes and the feelings that repeat themselves across market and decision sequences.

Now compare this information to what you discovered in step 4.

What seems similar?

Something should; in fact, for some people, it jumps off the page. For others, it doesn't immediately click, so if you find yourself in that situation, let it rattle around in the back of your brain for a few weeks. However, let's take a look at the kind of thing you might find.

"I never can get what I want."

"It is always my fault for …"

"If I had just been a little more careful or worked harder …"

"If I just didn't do the stupid things!"

This list could go on and on. One thing about fractal-emotional contexts is that while they are similar they are also like fingerprints. Everyone has one that is truly their own. The details differ from person to person.

But play each one out, or just an imaginary one you can come up with, as it would relate to taking a trade, being in a winning trade and deciding what to do or getting out of a losing trade. To do this, imagine: "What if I felt that way?" and "How would that feeling be acted out when I am in the midst of a decision I am very unsure about?"

For example, "I can never get what I want" might translate to a feeling and acting out of not letting winners run or getting out of trades too early. "It is always my fault" easily morphs into "I shouldn't have done that" and getting out of a trade almost immediately. "If I had been a little more careful" also leads to getting out early.

Exits are the tough part of trading because, as we discussed earlier, the potential for regret always looms as a relatively conscious-feeling context but these feelings above exacerbate that. And most of the time no one knows it! In fact, one of the ironies of trading is that winners almost always make you feel bad—either you didn't stay in long enough or you got out soon. We expect losers to make us feel bad but we fail to realize that winners ironically usually put us in a "no-win" situation in terms of our satisfaction with the result.

The Independent Money Manager's "Blocked" Fractal

On the other hand, occasionally, a trader calls us who wants to know why they seem to not have the ability to take a trade at all. Of course, these callers trade their own money, but over the years I have run into more than one who has sat in front of a screen for years, can usually explain the market quite well, and yet can't actually put money at "risk."

In one case, recently, I worked with an exceptionally nice man with whom we figured out together had a rather complex multifractal (many zigs and zags in a core pattern of emotional experience). I can happily report that unraveling what his repetitive experience was helped him deal with market decisions in a completely new way, one that worked much better than his old way.

He came from a very unusual family situation. His parents didn't speak to each other for years, even though they lived under the same roof. His childhood consisted of relaying messages back and forth and sitting through endless completely silent dinners. And as you can imagine, his parents both attempted to curry more of his favor. He grew up being pulled in two directions every moment of his life.

At first I didn't see it but then it hit me. Any trade has the potential regret tree. As we recently discussed, no matter what you do in the majority of your trades, you could have always done better—let run longer, got out sooner, or just taken the money and run. In short, after working on this issue for a few months we realized that the pro/con argument for any market decision mimicked his previous situation with his parents. Any reasons to buy (and the feeling contexts in place) took on the role of one parent and the reasons not to buy or to sell unconsciously took on the role of the other. No matter how much he understood what was happening in the market or no matter how much confidence he had that he had "seen this movie before," it didn't matter. The completely unconscious emotional fractal operating was an exact repetition built of the two transferences—one stemming from his mother and one originating with his father—of his childhood. Amazingly, this went on for years, which while again astonishing, isn't really when you remember that his brain was wired to fire within this context. So what solved the problem?

The classic Freudian viewpoint says that the interpretation or that just by realizing the trade was not really a re-creation of his parents' push-pull dynamic will solve the problem. Other schools working with psychoanalytic theory have found it much more effective to create a new emotional experience. Given that you have to have a feeling to actually take any action, we somehow had to work with the feeling—on the feeling level—in order for him to be able to implement a market decision and not be stuck going back and forth forever between the pros and cons of a given situation (like how he was stuck forever going back and forth between his parents).

The Ironic Solution to Fractal Contexts

As is often the case, the solution to creating a new emotional experience almost always means going *with* whatever feeling is in place. This means stopping the effort to use your intellect to talk yourself out of feeling and doing what is called "joining" it—or going along with it, at least in your mind.

So one week, I gave him the assignment of imagining that the reasons for and against the trade were being argued by his mother and father, respectively. We made the unconscious context both conscious and felt.

A couple of weeks went by and sure enough, he found that by putting the feeling context into the here and now, he was actually able to work with the underlying feeling. In turn, their power to be unknowingly acted out dissipated, and he actually took a trade!

Now believe me, I know that seems almost impossible. But I have seen this kind of thing over and over.

Renee was actually having a little trouble following this. "Denise, are you saying that instead of using his intellect or cognitive capacity to remind himself that the two sides of the trading argument were not literally his mother and father, you asked him to do the opposite? Most people would try to remind themselves about reality, right? But if I follow you, you are saying that a kind of play acting that demonstrates the underlying feelings can be more effective. Is that correct?"

That's basically it, Renee. It really boils down to feeling the unconscious feeling context so that the energy of the feeling is occurring in the present. They call it "joining the resistance," where resistance means an intellectual defense against awareness of the repetition or recreation of an earlier experience. Let me give you another example.

A few weeks ago, I worked with a trader at a multibillion dollar hedge fund that traded a purely discretionary strategy. He had recently been given more capital and instructions from the chief investment officer to "hit the ball out of the park." Of course, you might be able to guess how well he had been doing since that admonition—not great. We talked about how he really felt, that he was trying too hard and kept telling himself not to but it wasn't working. He had even taken on more risk in his personal account, which normally he was exceptionally conservative about.

I told him what I wanted him to do was go back to his desk and really feel the feeling of hitting the ball out of the park. Really try to do it—put on more size and swing for the proverbial fences. He looked at me like I had just grown an insect out of my forehead, but within a moment he laughed and said, "But then I would probably take off risk!" In other words, as soon as he allowed himself to feel what he really felt, as opposed to trying to talk himself out of it, his emotions changed. He felt differently about what he wanted to do. Using your head to talk yourself out of the feelings you have just doesn't work very well, if at all. It might look on the surface as if it does, but the feeling will linger and reappear, oftentimes acted out instead of just felt. Leaning into the feelings or fully experiencing them without any judgment about whether they are the right way to feel or whether you want to feel that way has this ironic effect of disrupting the feeling.

In this case, wanting to hit the ball out of the park makes perfect sense. Who wouldn't want to? Actually doing so may be near impossible, but that doesn't make the feeling wrong. Simply put, that feeling is motivation and working with it in a different way allows it to have a positive impact.

Perceptual Realities

You might not want to see it. You might not be able to see it. Most traders can't *fully* figure it out, at least at this level of detail. But I guarantee you that for each one of you, I can figure out the match between your personal history and your emotional experiences in trading. I have never, in all my years of coaching, been unable to find a trader's repetition, assuming he or she gives me the data. Most of the time, I can do it backwards—I hear of a problem, such as being able to make money for a long stretch and then inexplicably giving it back, and I have a fairly good idea of what life generally was like for the trader when they were a child.

I am not saying that to pat myself on the back. I am saying it to convince you that it is there and, in turn, motivate you to do the detective work. It's worth every bit of psychic discomfort the process might bring for that first moment when you avoid your next worst trade of the year because you had the knowledge and the understanding of how to act out of a different feeling context than one that was imbued into you.

Resistance

A subject we must touch on, although it is far from my favorite, is the very real resistance to knowing or feeling what we feel, either the surface feelings or certainly the fractal ones. Many times we would all like to leave well enough alone. Sometimes even certain types of psychologists will tell you to do so. It seems that particularly in these days of designer drugs, it appears so much easier to just take a pill as opposed to resolve the underlying and unconscious fractal-emotional context.

It is true that most of these feelings don't feel that good. I was never that fond of figuring out that my biological mother gave me up and then turned around and had another daughter only 18 months later. I didn't think it bothered me because my parents, the real ones who raised me, gave me so much more than it appeared she could have—a better education and exposure to so much more of the world. For most of us, such stuff got buried for a reason—self-protection at the time of the original experience and perception. To excavate the feelings brings up *pain*. It just seems much easier to live without that pain. And plenty of cognitively trained psychologists will tell you it won't do any good to go there anyway. So, why bother?

But see here is the rub—you are tricking yourself. The multifractal and simple fractal self-perceptions and expectations *are* being acted on.

But we tend to like what has defended us in the past. Defense mechanisms, the roots of not knowing, worked for us as children. They kept us mentally safe and motivated. If something goes wrong when you are little and you literally have no power, it makes you feel as if you do (have power) to say "oh, it is my fault." Think about it; if it is your fault then it lies within your purview to do something about it. This is actually called the narcissistic defense.

In adulthood, these explanations and expectations hold us back. They function more like keeping a caterpillar from becoming a butterfly. A silk cocoon seems to have its advantages but, really, how does it compare to the free flight of a butterfly?

The Terror of Being Lost in Home Depot

How does a two year old feel in general? Can you remember? I know that neither Michael nor Renee have young children but what about the rest of you? Think back to some of your earliest memories or, if you can't remember, conjecture. As young children, don't we all feel totally dependent on the adults, or otherwise helpless? Aren't we all scared "out of our mind" if we wander off from our mothers in the grocery store? Can you get a sense, a visceral memory of that level of fear?

In a way, the market again makes us all feel exactly that way, on one day or another. The Monday after the S&P downgrade in August 2011 put everyone into a situation where they had no context of any kind—factual or emotional—and as such was a very nerve-wracking day for many even very experienced professionals. Or, it might have been the Flash Crash, October 2008 or August 2007. If you were around, it might have been in October 1997 or 1987, the days when what seems to be the norm comes unglued, because it does. The glue—the general rhythm, range, and speed—goes haywire.

Probabilistically speaking, it is the path to "all correlations go to 1." Contextually speaking and on the surface, it depends on what came before; but feeling-context wise, it returns all of us to fractals of childhood. For a moment, or much longer, we have *no* idea what to do.

We do everything we can to avoid this feeling of falling into an abyss. We add charts and news analysis and now machines whose operators purport to have taught them to learn through ostensibly life-like neural networks. We might, however, want to consider simply feeling this feeling consciously and intentionally. Think of it as battle training—if we are familiar with the feeling context, then we will have a better idea what to do when it strikes. If we are not, and you can say this about every feeling, we will just act it out. We will buy or sell at the worst moment.

Normally, we think we act out when the pain is too great, and that may be true to an extent. I submit to you it is actually when the uncertainty is too great and we imagine the pain.

And yes, I know, Home Depot can scare the heck out of anyone, at any age. Either you have no clue what to do with all of this stuff or you have no clue how you are going to do everything the person with you is planning as you walk down the aisles.

Chapter 18

Is That an Impulse or Is It Implicit Knowledge?

blink?
Coup d'État Capital Monthly Workshop
November 12, 2012

Thank you Michael, Renee, and Chris for getting your whole team together for this month's workshop. In order to pull together everything we've been working on, I would like to use this month's meeting to talk a bit about how to know when a feeling is an impulse imbued with fractal fuel or when it is what we commonly refer to as intuition but we should think of as experiential knowledge.

We've never specifically focused on this but the question is: "Is a certain physical feeling mosaic Malcolm Gladwell's 'blink,' or does it just feel that way in the moment?"

Behavioral finance can produce research showing that we find patterns where there are none, but we all also know that sometimes we just "know." The trick is learning how to tell the difference!

What Is Implicit Learning, Intuition, or Unconscious Pattern Recognition?

I suggest we begin with thinking about what the phenomenon of "just knowing" actually is. Intuition, as it's usually called, is that knowledge communicated via a feeling that stems from having seen something before and recognizing the details at a level below awareness. I like to call it unconscious pattern recognition or tacit knowledge (a term used in a 2008 intuition study done at the University of Sweden).

Consider it the difference between knowledge learned in a book and knowledge built through doing and experiencing. Think of it this way—what differs between a brand new MBA and someone with years of trading desk experience? The recent graduate might have more technical knowledge but that book knowledge has no feeling attached to it. It's a case of knowing something only theoretically. Without experience, one lacks the sense, which is of course a type of feeling context, of how things fit together or whether they are true or false. The Swedish study quoted skiing champion Ingemar Stenmark as saying, "My legs think faster than I do" and Wayne Gretsky now famously saying, "Skate where the puck's going, not where it's been." The study also documented work done with physicians and business people in the 1990s that of course showed how people with experience perform better than those without.

In 2009, *The New York Times* published an article called "In Battle, Hunches Prove to be Valuable." The article recounted a nine-man team going out on patrol in Mosul, Iraq, one horridly hot summer morning and just barely avoiding a bomb explosion because their leader leveraged this "I just know" feeling. One of the soldiers had wanted to approach a car with two school-age boys inside to give them water. Something told the leader, "No, something isn't right" and sure enough, within moments, the car exploded. The situation had been arranged to draw the soldiers in. When the sergeant tried to recount what he saw, he had trouble, but he also said, "My body suddenly got cooler: you know, that danger feeling ... I can't point to one thing ..."

The army has done all kinds of work on intuition and says "that the speed with which the brain reads and interprets sensations like the feelings in one's own body and emotions in the body language of others is central to avoiding imminent threat." An army psychologist said some fighters can become very sensitive to small changes, i.e., they learn to realize, to hear the feeling signal. It's not the conventional wisdom of ignoring how you feel; it is honing your awareness of it. Their research found that under threatening situations the Green Berets and Navy SEALs experience the *same* avalanche of brain chemicals as regular recruits but their levels plummet more quickly. I think their psyches are satisfied with the intra-psychic communication, if you will. Once the more influential departments in our minds are sure the operations department (what we think of as our conscious knowledge) has received the message, they move onto other things.

Another 2008 study showed how experienced people make decisions faster. The author said that our unconscious builds a picture book that it sorts through to reference. When it finds a match—voilà!—you get that feeling. That feeling that can occur any time, such as the other day when I was talking with one of my other hedge fund clients and he said, "You know, Denise, sometimes I am getting coffee and get a feeling about what the market is going to do. But then I get in front of the screen and start reading my research and I don't listen to it. Then at the end of the day, I kick myself because it was right—and I didn't listen!"

Ideally, all of our work is to bring you to a place where you can distinguish between the feeling my other client speaks of and other kind of feelings. In other words, all of our work points toward having confidence in knowing when that body-brain-mind phenomenon of experiential knowledge is speaking.

Chris looked at Michael, Renee and the others as he chimed in, "Yes gang, this is really a differentiator. It is so hard to put words around but it is real. I think what Denise is saying is that science is now showing it to be something much more than our imaginations and I for one am glad we are talking about systematically approaching the topic. In my experience, the traders who value experiential knowledge (that is the term you used, right Denise?) have an edge over those who remain in their intellect."

Non-Deliberate Complex Decisions

Yes Chris, our brain can assemble tiny details in nanoseconds. It delivers a feeling to our consciousness that we can't intentionally access with the same speed. It's almost as if when we think about it, we are taking up precious time in our brains. In fact, another group of studies suggests that "deliberation without attention" brings better results than conscious linear thought. In four different cases, people reviewing the outcomes of more complex decisions were happier with the results when they made their choice without "attentive deliberation." This is another reason it pays to walk away from your market screens or your research and intentionally not think about it. Let your unconscious go to work on the data and deliver to you a better answer. Sometimes if you are a trader, it is enough to just leave for coffee and then when it is poured, ask yourself, what's my best decision?

Experiential Knowledge Versus Fractal Fuel

Unfortunately, learning these things isn't something you do in a day. Think of it more like learning a sport, maybe not as difficult as golf, but training and re-training your mind-body integration.

Look for these differentiators. ***If a feeling feels urgent, if it feels compelling, suspect it as impulse.*** If on the other hand, it feels calm, if it is a sense coming out of nowhere, consider it as recognition of something you know but aren't conscious of yet.

I realize the difference may be subtle and the rule surely isn't foolproof. But it is a very good practical start that if you can remember to employ, will save you a handful of impulsive entries or exits a month or a year.

Second, get in the habit of checking for the repeat of your fractal-feeling context.

What we often experience as a "given" really is just that script, those unconscious expectations, playing out. If we can recognize the fractal feelings and actually verbalize them, we have a good shot at extracting them from the decision context we are working in. For each time we can do so, we make a better decision.

In fact, a few years ago, a client of mine in Europe began to track every little nuance of his feelings on a spreadsheet, after some time and a lot of work, he said he knew when the feeling was his experiential learning, and he could trust it to be more than 90% accurate in terms of predicting short-term moves in the market.

Obviously, that is where you all want to get to, right? The trick is committing to the course, continuing in the track you all are already on of valuing emotional capital and managing psychological leverage. You appreciate that you won't "arrive," you will just get better and better at it.

I assure you though, the more you work at it, the more the results will reveal themselves to your bottom line. And sometimes, don't forget, "working on it" means doing nothing conscious. Just like the old trading saying, "no position, is a position," intentionally letting your mind wander should be a strategy. Your feelings might sort themselves out, complex decisions might get made, and all of your deliberate training just might come out to play!

When You Don't Know How You Feel

Sometimes some of us truly don't know and can't seem to find out how we feel no matter how hard we try. We have spent many years working on not knowing how we feel and it worked.

Let me share a few ideas from Lauren Smith, a teacher trained in the philosophy of Rudolf Steiner. Steiner believed in learning by using the whole psyche and is the forefather of Waldorf schools where children don't only do problems, they get up and play games where they are adding and subtracting. They may, at a very elementary level, have their art class be an assignment to draw the numbers (like the alphabet paintings by the art-deco icon Erté).

You want to acquire knowledge of your whole self—the complete body-brain-mind continuum, right? So it makes sense to start with the body, as that is easier than digging into a mind that closed itself off from feeling. Things you do primarily with your body can help you to access how you feel. A sport obviously comes to mind but go down another slightly different road that involves more sensory and solitary factors. Music, artwork, and poetry may certainly seem completely unrelated to markets but they of course are not. For one, with music, you can liken it to the speeds and rhythms of the way things move—is it jazz or classical or rap? But listening to it can help you relate to a song, and then if you like the words, you can assume you feel something like what the lyrics are talking about. Creating your own artwork, gardening, or poetry can also make it easier to hear yourself, if you are listening.

In 2010 I did a workshop where I asked the group of traders to write a story, poem, song, or essay about their distaste for ambiguity (the Ellsberg paradox that shows we prefer known probabilities to unknown). There were about a dozen people in the class and they all said, at first, that they thought it was a weird homework assignment; but as they did it, they really felt how much they detested the fact that they couldn't know the real probabilities. They felt it, and once they consciously felt it, it became easier to remember and to circumvent their acting on it in real time.

The Relationship of Intellect to Feelings

All this discussion and contemplation of your mental states is meant to teach you to work on an emotional level as a market advantage. The strategies and tactics aren't about using your intellect beyond turning your attention to your emotional capital. In other words, don't tell yourself to feel differently. Feel what you feel and use your intellect to allow yourself to feel more of it. Use your intellect to describe and analyze it. Use your brain to put words to it. And then just keep on doing it. Like the client I mentioned who knew a certain feeling had a 92% chance of being right—that is where you are ultimately trying to get, to know the difference between a fractal-fueled fear of missing out and tacit, implicit, or experiential knowledge.

As you get to know the difference, you can use the awareness of a certain type of emotional context to make a risk management choice or a strategy choice. You can be assured that you will be working with your perceptional mechanisms the way they were meant to work and as such, your perceptions will gradually improve. You will be able to trust that change in how your body feels to the benefit of what you thought was just an intellectual game.

Denise needn't say more. Michael could see the difference between impulse and intuition, recognizing his various feeling states.

Chapter 19

Run Over

Monday, August 11, 2014

As Michael fought his bedspread to find his jangling phone, he could see the clock glowing a painful 12:55 AM.

"Who the hell is calling me now?

"Is this Michael Kelley?

"Yes it is."

"Do you have a brother named Tom Kelley in Aspen, Colorado?

"Yes, who is this, please?"

"Mr. Kelley, I am Dr. Michelle Kmecik calling from Aspen Mountain Hospital. Tom was in an accident tonight. He is stable now but in critical condition."

Michael bolted up in bed. "What happened?!"

"As best we understand it, sir, he was riding his bike at dusk coming back into town and as he made the s-curve, he was hit from behind. He was wearing a helmet but nevertheless suffered a concussion, a broken tibia and fibula, which we have surgically repaired, and as there is bruising, it appears that his abdomen made contact with the handlebars so we are watching his spleen and pancreas closely. Are you his closest relative?"

"Well, yes ... uh ... well, no, I mean our parents are alive but he and my father don't speak."

"I see. Well, Tom needs a family member here so I must urge you to call them and figure out who can get here the soonest. He is stable but critical."

"Uh, sure, of course. Who are you again? Who do we contact?"

"My name is Michelle Kmecik. I am the emergency room physician on call tonight."

"Ok. Thank you, Dr. Kmecik. No wait—can I talk to him?"

"I am sorry, Mr. Kelley. He is still sedated. Please let the nursing station know approximately when a family member will arrive. Let me give you their direct line. Do you have a pen?"

"This can't be happening," thought Michael. "Crap! I have so many positions on and I am the only one who understands them." Between the second ratings downgrade of US debt in a little over a year and China's severe recession, the perfect storm for global bond and gold markets had been brewing for weeks.

"But I *have* to go," Michael thought. "This is serious and no one else can help. Surely Renee can help me manage the positions." She had been building an options hedge for them anyway.

Michael decided he needed to call their mother, even though it was 11 on the West Coast and he knew she would be sleeping. He filled her in on what happened and mentioned that someone had to get to Aspen ASAP.

"Michael, I can't get to LAX at this hour. Can you get the first flight out?"

"Yes, I am going to try. It's just that, well, I don't know if you have been paying any attention to the markets lately but … well, obviously Tom needs us—and I really do want to go. I am just trying to figure out how to while I also deal with my own kind of serious jam here at work. Plus, we have to call Dad."

"Michael, I can't call him. I haven't spoken to him in eight years!"

"Yeah, Mom, but Tom is a son to both of you," said Michael as calmly as he could possibly muster.

"Yes, yes … but you are the only one who talks to him at all! And you know how he will react—the doctors don't have a clue, he has to step in… . You know."

"Okay, okay, I will call him before I board the plane. There is nothing he can do from Connecticut at this hour anyway."

Michael stuffed a bag with a change of clothes and his laptop and then realized he had just enough time to go by the office for the London open and make a 6 AM flight to Denver out of O'Hare. He'd call the airlines from the taxi.

* * *

As he stared at his screens in the middle of the night, he at first thought he was seeing things. Treasuries were down, the dollar was down, equities were down, and gold wasn't really up. This was bizarre.

Everything was going against him. Surely this must just be because the markets were thin. It was a Monday morning and maybe it was just a fire-sale buying opportunity? Maybe I should just add, just this once. That will lower my average price and I'll be more protected while I am on the plane and out of touch, he rationalized as he tapped out a few key strokes.

* * *

Renee, who had officially joined the firm just a month ago, came into the office earlier than usual. She'd woken up at 5 AM and with all of the economic news breaking she knew she couldn't go back to sleep. As she put her key into the lock, she noticed the lights were on. And then the door was unlocked. "Wow, this is weird. Who has been here?"

Michael's desk was a mess, which she found supremely odd. He had a neat-nick streak and kept his desk orderly but now newspapers and printer paper laid everywhere.

As she grabbed her cell phone to call Michael, she realized she had left it on vibrate and she had a text: "Tom's been hurt. On my way to Aspen. Call you when I land." And then a second one: "See what you can do with the book. Everything was against me in the middle of the night."

"What's he talking about? Is he kidding?" she thought. It was his book. He only gave her a broad idea of his themes. "I'm not a directional trader," she thought.

She decided to check their prime broker's trade log and what she saw surprised, even stunned, her. Michael had added to two losing positions at 3:47 AM. "That wasn't like him," she thought. "And he had broken one of their cardinal rules. Now the losses were getting even worse."

She felt her phone rumble. "Ree — don't have much time — have to sprint to get to the Aspen gate. What's the market doing?"

"Michael, did you add to these positions in the middle of the night?" She asked in a clipped tone.

"Yes. This is crazy — it's an over-reaction in a thin market. Why — are we down more?" asked Michael.

"Yep … it doesn't look good."

"Ree, this is a once in a decade opportunity. Can you add some more for me? I won't have time to get logged on and make the plane."

"I thought you wanted me to hedge them," she said in an unusually deep voice.

"I do! But I also want you to add to the core longs."

"Michael, you aren't serious, are you? Isn't that breaking one of the few rules we have? Don't add to losers. You always say it is trying to force the rest of the world to see the market your way — you know that!"

"Ree, this is different. Half of this move might simply be the thin summer markets. It will be okay. I've got to go, but we will be fine."

Michael hung up, exasperated. Tom needed him, and he wanted to go, but it was the worst time. He had never really been trading when markets had become this violent and he really needed to be at his desk to see the speed and rhythm of how things were moving.

"Oh geez, I promised Mom I would call Dad," he realized. As they loaded more bags into the puddle-jumper to Aspen, Tom reluctantly tapped "RK office" in his call log; even though he would surely be in the middle of his morning meeting with the CEO of the insurance company. He probably wouldn't even answer.

When he did, Michael stumbled, "Dad, uh listen, I'm in Denver on my way to Aspen. Tom got hit by a car last night while riding his bike and the hospital called me around 1."

"What? What are you talking about, Michael?"

"What do you mean what I am talking about?" said Michael before with clear agitation he repeated, "Tom got hit a by a car while riding his bike and he is in the hospital in Aspen. The doctor who called asked for a family member to get there as soon as possible, so I got the first flight out and am now almost there."

"Why did they call you? And more importantly, why didn't you call me?" barked Richard with more than a few excessive decibels.

"It was the middle of the night, and you are at least almost three hours farther away!"

"Michael, exactly what did they say?"

"That he was stabilized but still in critical condition."

"Look, I do have to go. The flight attendants are pointing at my phone."

Richard hung up feeling a jolt of a feeling that he hadn't felt in years. Tom was hurt and Michael would never know how to handle the doctors. If there was one thing Richard knew it was that doctors needed managing! If you didn't take matters into your own hands, mistakes always got made. Maybe his friend Bill Riley would let him use his Marquette Air hours. That would get him there faster before Michael made the situation worse.

* * *

As Michael sat dozing by Tom's bedside he was stunned to hear his father's booming voice. He hadn't reached the room but Michael could hear him saying, "But, doctor, I want you to tell me exactly what his prognosis is?"

"How did he get here so fast?" Michael wondered.

"Shhhh!" hissed a nurse to Richard. "Mr. Kelley needs rest!"

Tom's condition was still critical as described, but he appeared to be resting comfortably. Dr. Kmecik had said something about a careful watch for a possible slow bleed from the spleen. Michael felt helpless to do anything other than sit there. Richard of course probably felt as if he needed to tell the doctors what to do. With barely a hello, he took his father's sudden arrival as a chance to go outside and call the office. Like all hospitals, mobile phones were frowned upon so he hadn't checked the markets in more than two hours. He just knew there had to be a reversal—this wasn't 2008 after all.

"Ree, what's up?"

"Well, things don't look so great. Geithner is again saying this second US debt downgrade is meaningless but rumors are swirling that China really is a seller of Treasuries this time."

"Oh, c'mon, they can't sell without hurting themselves. Besides they are known to have a five-year plan to generate more internal GDP and they are only three years into it. I think, if anything, they could behind schedule given the recession they seem to be in."

"Yeah, I know that and you know that, but evidently not everyone else does."

"Renee, please just add some more. This thing is all out of whack because it is a summer Monday and half of Wall Street is still in the Hamptons. I know I am right about this one."

"Michael, I really don't think so. My options overlays aren't doing us much good, and we seem to be standing smack in front of a steamroller."

"Look, I've studied the charts. There are so many high volume areas below, it just has to hold. Those long-term holders will step in and buy there. I just know it."

"Michael, my father would never trade that way!" she retorted with immediate regret. She wished she could take it back. She knew Michael needed to prove himself, sometimes a little too much for some inexplicable reason, but she really didn't mean to deliver that low of a blow.

"Whoa … your father would never trade that way?" Michael felt as if he had been punched in the gut by a very big man instead of a lithe, female volleyball player.

"Michael, I'm sorry—I really didn't mean it the way it sounds.…"

"Never mind, I will just call Josh at Newline. He is always saying we don't work him hard enough for the prime brokerage commission we pay so now I can. He will trade my account as I ask. He'll see the opportunity. The Chinese aren't really going to sell any of their US debt holdings. It is all talk. So the markets are oversold. Plus, we could be up over 25%, maybe even 50%, if it works. That would be our best year to date. When we start to raise outside capital next year those kinds of numbers on the boards would look really good."

"Sounds like what Denise always calls fear of missing out, if you ask me … or needing to be right."

"Look I have to get back upstairs before Richard irritates any more of the staff" said Michael as he hung up without waiting for a response.

Thank God Tom was at least stable. The doctors were saying it would take 36 hours to be sure about the spleen and the pancreas. Their mother was about to arrive. He hated to leave. He knew Tom didn't need their father terrorizing the doctors or to even see him when he woke up, but Coup d'État was really Michael's whole life. They had some junior analysts and execution traders now, but having been laid off from trading desks twice, this was going to be his last chance.

"Dad, I think now that with you and Mom here, I am going to try to get back to Chicago tonight. The markets are crazy with all this debt talk and it is just too hard to manage from here."

"You are going to do what!?!! Rush right back to that money-grubbing operation of yours while your brother's life hangs in the balance," growled Richard.

"Dad, they said he was stable. And Mom will be here in less than an hour. She's already landed."

"But you are the one who can stay up and monitor him at all hours. I am too old for that. Can't you do what you need to do from here?"

"Things are moving too fast. I need to be back."

"The only place you need to be is here. And that's my final word!" yelled Richard loudly enough to startle the nurses at the desk four rooms away.

*   *   *

He didn't feel like calling the office. Renee would probably just harass him over the positions. Josh would give him an update without judgment.

"Really, what do you think?" Michael asked his prime broker.

"Well, man, I don't know, you've got a big position here, I might cut it."

"Really, I was thinking of adding to it. None of this makes any sense—China can't really sell and the Fed and Treasury will certainly step in. The dollar can't just keep getting hammered like this. In fact, yeah, I am sure of this. Just buy some more 10 years, Apple, Google, and LinkedIn."

"Are you sure, man?

"Yes, and while you are at it add 5,000 e-mini 'spoos' too."

Over his father's objections, Michael did make it back to Denver and onto another overnight flight—first west and now east—in a little over 24 hours. He went straight to the office despite desperately needing a shower and shave. Normalcy would have to wait. He had to see all his markets together.

He saw that the usual relationships of late between US Treasuries and gold were *not* holding. Both were down. The fund had given back 25% of their gains for the year.

Surely this had to turn around later today. Back in October 1997, the Dow was down 500 points on Monday afternoon and came roaring back on Tuesday. In 2011, there was that week where it was up or down 400 net points for four days in row. These kinds of swift moves and subsequent reactions happened much more frequently, but time after time, the market comes back. This should be the same. It wasn't banks again going broke, after all. As he sat blankly staring at the screen, the phone rang.

"Michael Kelley speaking."

"I thought you would like to know the doctors just upgraded him to serious," Richard said.

"That's terrific, Dad. Is he awake?"

"No. But actually the real reason I called is that I want to know why you defied me and left."

"Dad, I have responsibilities. I have other people's money under my watch. I am the only one that can really manage our portfolios. We are still small and no one else here can do what I do."

"You choose your greed over your brother!"

Michael started to say, "Dad it isn't like that …"—but Richard had hung up.

"This is impossible," thought Michael. "I can't be in two places at once. What does he want me to do—quit? Fail?"

As he turned to his screen he saw that the S&P had taken another dip. It was nearing the overnight low. It should hold here. This would be the perfect time to buy at one last lower price. As he pushed the buttons again, Renee appeared at his door.

"Whoa, you're wiped. You need sleep!"

"I got some on the plane, but I can't sleep with these markets moving the way they are."

"Actually, Michael, you can't afford not to. You know you can't make a decent decision without sleep. You know that you won't judge the risk properly! We've always had that as our first rule of managing our psychological leverage," argued Renee.

"I'm okay, trust me, I am fine."

"Yeah that's what it always looks like when you are too tired to know it," Renee uncharacteristically snapped.

Michael just sat there. On one hand, he had that adrenaline-filled energy and on the other, thinking seemed like a chore. He felt a hundred things and he felt nothing. It was almost like he was outside of himself. His positions were huge, and he was risking a lot. Tom seemed okay but maybe he wasn't. Renee, who had never been short-tempered with him, clearly was exasperated. And his father ... well, it was always the same — never good enough, never the right thing.

As he stared at the screen through some sort of dense haze, he realized that in fact that all the markets were bouncing. Maybe he really was right after all? Everyone was coming to their senses and seeing the buying opportunity he had seen earlier. This was going to be a killer trade.

If he went home right now for a shower, shave, and an hour's nap, he could be back by the regular hours close.

* * *

Tuesday, 2:00 PM

As Michael locked up his bike, he saw Chris's Mercedes parked at the corner. That's odd, he thought. This would be maybe only the third time he had come in during the summer in two years. That first summer, 2012, he came in at least weekly and stayed the day; but last year, he came in maybe once, and that was to pick up a check.

Inside, he didn't see Renee or Chris as he sat down in front of his screens.

"What? This can't be right." The fund had lost 8% more since he left three hours ago. "No way! That just can't be," Michael said to himself under his breath. As he did, he realized someone was walking up behind him. He turned to see Chris.

"Michael, these positions are quite large, and at the moment, quite against us. Can you tell me about your rationale?"

"Well, Chris," he said (thinking maybe he should be calling him Mr. Smith), "These markets are way oversold. Everyone's assuming the worst but there is no way that China will start massively selling US Treasuries. They can't afford to. So this rumor just should not be pushing bond prices to where they are."

"Yes, Michael, but the fund is down by over 32% from where we were just a few weeks ago. When we started I basically gave you free rein, but you need to start closing out, and closing out quickly."

"But ..."

"No, Michael," Chris said in a tone he had never heard him use. "I am not asking, I am telling. Get out now!" And then the man who put him in business turned and walked away.

Chapter 20

The "What Was I Thinking" Rehash

"Michael, what exactly happened?" asked Denise as they sat in the brick-walled conference room in Coup d'État's office. No one else was around at this late hour, so it was a good time to analyze what happened.

"I was just *so* sure the market would bounce. It was a late summer Monday morning! The markets were just too thin due to vacations, not due to a total lack of interest. Or at least that's what I thought," Michael replied with a look of embarrassment.

"Okay. I can understand that. But let's think about what seems to have happened psychologically?"

"Well, my book seemed more or less well positioned when I left on Friday. Sunday there were rumors about some talk out of China but then when I got the call about my brother, my mind seemed to go into hyper-drive. I felt so strongly that I needed to get to Aspen but that I also needed to be at my desk I guess that the urgency I felt about Tom seeped into my feelings the market. It's kind of hard to deconstruct it actually."

"Well I do think you are onto something there. Let's look at the trades in sequential order. Maybe we can reconstruct the psychological timeline."

"Well, I went into the office on the way to the airport; the markets were down so I thought it was thin and I would be safe to add to a loser, at least once. The volume and price clusters I look at would normally have held in the social context of an unsubstantiated rumor in the middle of August. Normally, a lot of traders would read that as an opportunity to buy on an extreme over-reaction."

"Okay, what next?" asked Denise while consciously trying to avoid any tone of judgment.

Michael paused and looked out the window.

"Thinking back on it, I am not sure what happened while I was in Aspen. I just felt so strongly about adding again. I guess … oh, I don't know … it was like something came over me. Traders talk about their demons and, well…now I kind of get it. I feel like I know better, so it's hard to explain really why I made the choices I did. I felt an inkling that maybe the positions were getting too big but the upside potential seemed too good to walk away from. And God knows, the last thing I wanted to do was get out at the bottom!"

"I understand. So now you are in Aspen at the hospital, right? Was your father there yet?" asked Denise.

"Upstairs. I had used his arrival to get outside and check on the markets. I know you believe in these things you call fractal psyches, but why does his behavior now matter? He hates what I do and the whole idea of trading anyway."

"Yes, I understand. Our fractal feelings (and their resulting perceptions and compelled reactions) have a way most strongly asserting their influence at the worst moments. The individual elements or simple fractals of our expectations and feelings get rolled together like a cookie recipe that turns into a repetitive experience. After some time passes, we can see we weren't really responding to what was happening in the moment but to an emotional context emerging from another time in our lives."

"Fair enough," said Michael as he again shifted his eyes to the window. "Let me think … I can't remember exactly how long he had been there when he said that I was the one who needed to stay with Tom. In fact, he didn't ask me, he ordered me."

"Really … that seems a bit overbearing, wouldn't you say?"

"Well, yes, but typical Richard Kelley style."

"You've told me he looks down on your trading and is generally critical of just about everyone. What feelings did his behavior induce in you?"

"Not sure I know what you mean by induce, Denise."

"Good question. A person acts a certain way and that in essence 'gives' us certain constellations or mosaics of feelings. We wouldn't have them without interacting with that person."

"Well … for one, he made it seem like he even showed up there because he thought I couldn't handle it. I mean he borrowed, bought, I don't know, expensive jet hours to get there—and this is after not speaking to Tom for years! That certainly made me feel as if he were afraid I would somehow make the wrong decision and Tom would be worse off. But he always has made me feel incompetent and unimportant so that wasn't anything particularly new."

"Okay. I think I understand, but what's the story behind his behavior towards Tom?" asked Denise. "I mean, not speaking to him. That seems quite extreme."

"Yes. He used to clearly favor him, but then he missed making the US Olympic ski team by one spot. Richard blamed Tom. He accused him of staying out too late partying the night before. He even blamed me for letting him, but, in fact, I was with him and he was home by 10. Dad didn't completely stop talking to him then. It was the next year when instead of going back to get his MBA he went to Aspen to patrol, Dad got so angry and, in effect, seemed to have disowned him—until now."

"So Richard is extraordinarily judgmental, right?

That's got to impact you. Are there other details or nuances in how he typically makes you feel?"

"Well, he acts like, and basically says that, what I do is criminal. He doesn't realize the smarts it takes to do this, and he certainly wouldn't give me credit for them even if he did."

"So in general, is it fair to say that it seems as if he has no respect for you?" asked Denise. "What would make you feel as if you had some power in the situation?"

"I'm not sure what you mean."

"If you could have, what would have liked to have done or said to Richard?"

"Well, to go back home, stay out of it, and let Mom manage. I would also like for him to realize the dilemma I was in and how I really desperately wanted to be in two places. But of course he could never see that."

"Michael, can you remember how you felt after you had your broker enter that last order?"

"Oh man, there was so much going on! I don't know. It's so hard to parse and even harder to remember," answered Michael.

"Try for whatever comes to mind," said Denise.

"I was so unbelievably tired but also running on adrenaline. If I really think about it, I kind of recall a feeling a bit better though. It was sort of a feeling of relief, like the pressure was off, I guess. Yeah, that's it. I remember feeling excited and I guess you would say, stalwart that I was going to do what I wanted and not let him control me."

"Yes, Michael, that is what I expected. Can you see that both your father and the market were making you feel out of control? Neither would cooperate nor agree with your point of view. Does that sound like how it felt?"

"Well, yeah … I guess … now that you put it that way."

"Could there be a parallel?"

"What do you mean?"

"Wouldn't you say both your father and the markets were being judgmental and unfair?"

* * *

This meltdown occurred and got worse through psychological levers on more than one level.

The first one is easy—too many decisions made while you clearly were sleep deprived. I know how easy it is to forget. When you need to remember the importance of trading as a physical endeavor, it is also simultaneously the most difficult to do.

The second is the fear of missing out—the markets seemed oversold and you were acting out the fear that you would miss a chance to substantially outperform.

The third and most influential is the general feeling of having no power; I am sure when you got word about Tom, you felt helpless to do anything. Adding to the position gave you a feeling of some modicum of control.

But the pervasive and unconscious motivator was fighting back against your father's criticism and judgment with the "I'll show you Mr. Market, I will be right, and sooner or later you will have to admit it." In fact, this would have exacerbated the entire scenario; this is the biggest factor in what made you add both when in Aspen and again back in the office on Tuesday morning.

Haven't you told me in the past that one of the problems you would like to solve is getting stubborn? You can be assured that that trait, if you want to call it that, isn't *just* being stubborn. There is a fractal-emotional context that has been with you for a long time. Undoubtedly, it served you well in getting through challenging moments in school or fighting for the bank job or even being willing to take on this hedge fund challenge. In fact, when the pattern first starting coming together, I am sure it served you well. It is acting out anger, and if we do that consciously and intentionally, it can be our best ally. But when we are doing so without really knowing who or what we are trying to retaliate against, it tends neither to serve our best interests nor to make us money.

I can and have told you stories of traders who act out like this. You have heard me talk about some of them in my lectures—the guy whose father became embodied in his whole trading plan, the guy who was always fighting for the last tick because his mother had never let him have a new bike or basketball shoes, even though they had plenty of money … I could go on. But the questions are:

How do you recover?

How do you avert this kind of being "run over" in the future?

Chapter 21

Getting Back in the Game

The Coup d'État Capital Trader Training Manual
A note on the psychology of dealing with uncertainty

Recovery

Recovering in trading generally continues to be like recovering momentum on an athletic field, at least for those who don't really understand the leading edge of brain science. The intellect still is supposed to be in charge, as opposed to its real power or role which is, albeit surprisingly, only a small part of the overall picture.

In sports, everyone can see the drain or destruction and everyone has also seen amazing turnarounds, but who can describe it systematically? Fixing feelings, which is what momentum or negative-momentum stems from, with intellect (or at least intellectual coats of paint) rarely if ever really works. We all listen to the positive thinking advice and say to ourselves, "Yeah but ..." and "You don't understand my situation, it's much worse than you realize."

In fact, the reason I really got into consulting in the first place was to help people who had been very successful recover from one or another of the various meltdowns that can befall a trader, particularly one that has had to plow his or her way through all of the ineffective and even damaging intellectual advice.

The Smartest Move You Can Make Is to *Let Yourself Feel Disgusted*

In a new world where feelings and emotions count, step one turns out to be quite different than you would think. Ironically, the most helpful thing to do when you have blown it is to feel bad! It won't kill you, it won't even cause you to throw up (most of the time), but it will put your body in synch with your mind and your mind in synch with reality. If you have made one or a series of spectacularly stupid decisions, what else are you supposed to feel? Isn't feeling like a chump rational? You blew it so of course you should feel like crapola!

In other words, step one of recovery amounts to mourning. You are mourning the death of your capital and you are mourning the temporary death of your sanity. Believe me, the quickest way out of this is going to be to feel as bad as you feel, whatever that is, and let that be that.

And yes, I know the objection. It seems that if you let yourself feel something bad, that you will end up in the abyss of that feeling. Most of us don't. We allow the feeling and it passes. While it is passing, it points our minds and yes, even our intellects to areas where we can improve or learn. We also disrupt the acting out of the feeling.

Typically, men more than women want to "do" something and intentionally feeling whatever feelings exist doesn't seem like doing anything. (Even though it is.) Men tend to immediately ask, "What should I do?," where "do" involves some sort of deliberate physical movement. Many of my clients move first toward taking action and the action of consciously feeling something, maybe because it is internal and can be done sitting still, clearly doesn't seem like doing anything. In terms of understanding one's over-arching emotional context, taking action can prevent one from ever knowing what that context really is. It just doesn't make sense to literally do anything (take physical action) until you really understand what went wrong and you don't have a snowball's chance of understanding where your perception got so off track until you let yourself feel crummy—most of the time, for however long it takes. I know you have visions of half-empty pizza boxes and beer bottles strewn all over your office, but, even if that did happen, would it be so bad?

It might seem like this strategy catapults you into a deep, dark hole. All I can say is, trust me. It doesn't. I have given this exercise to many a trader, including one who sits as an managing director on a major bank trading desk and, in his case, the next time I talked to him, he didn't even remember feeling bad. Most of the time, if you have the courage to feel badly, get to the root of the feeling, and realize that x-y-z feeling or fractal-emotional context crept up on you without you knowing it, the feeling "pops" like a balloon. Even if it doesn't pop, it begins losing air like a tire going flat. The overwhelming sense of urgency begins to dissipate. As that energy goes away, it gets easier to see how the feeling, emotional, and social contexts—the conscious and previously unconscious—were coloring your beliefs and perceptions.

Bottom line: the debilitating part just won't last that long if you just let yourself feel *and* articulate it, even if only to a journal.

Some people will tell you to put a time limit on it. That is only because they fear what will happen if you don't. Trust your psyche, it will take care of you. Feeling bad has informational value. It leads you to be introspective, and while you are doing so, here are some questions to ask:

- **What was the feeling context and emotional context, the *f*C and *e*C?** Where were you on the spectrum between the fear of losing and the fear of missing out? You were definitely somewhere, and more often than not, the mistake you make will be on the right-hand side, at the fear of future regret.

- **What was the fractal-emotional context, the *F-eC*?** Of course this third one will take a little help to figure out, and even more diligence to manage. But it is manageable—set phone alerts, put up sticky notes, *talk about it*.

I can guarantee you that a psychological set-up exists in your trading that makes you feel like you felt when you were a child. It is all there. The simple and early fractals were there before you got to high school. They may become re-mixed somewhat and events from your teenage years may exacerbate them, but the roots go deep.

Whatever self-perception, set of beliefs and expectations, and explanations you came up with for your rightful place in the world, chances are the negative or limiting ones are just the narcissistic view of a child who, if they can jury-rig something into being their fault, gains a false sense of control over the situation.

Deal Directly With the Intensity

Frankly, when the feelings and emotions you are experiencing become the most intense, you can be assured that it is not really about the markets or the money. When the thing you need to do, get out or walk away, seems to be literally the hardest thing to do, you can be assured that what you are feeling has a fractal component. It mostly is not about the here and now. The sooner you can remember this, in the heat of the battle, the less trouble you will get into. It sounds hard to believe, I know, but realizing that the intensity of wanting to be right, frustration over being wrong, or fear of missing something emanates from your past dilutes enough of the physical energy embedded in the emotion and gives you a window through which to unravel it, as opposed to acting out (or trading) with the money you manage.

Understanding this internal data gives you an edge, the psychological leverage, that no one no one can take away.

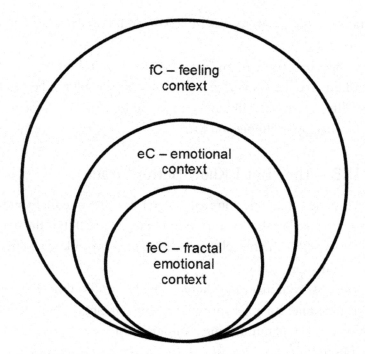

fC – feeling
context

eC – emotional
context

feC – fractal
emotional
context

Figure 21.1. Contexts diagram.

This diagram moves from the most conscious to the most unconscious elements of the feeling and emotional contexts. The feeling contexts include the basic physical feelings like tired and hungry. The emotional refers to the relatively easy to get at fears on the spectrum we have discussed. The innermost circle parallels your unconscious psyche, the fractal-emotional contexts or the transferences and repetitions of psychoanalytic theory.

Yes, there will always be time lags of varying degrees in how soon you realize it. But if you are managing to the objective of creating and maintaining psychological capital *first*, you will recognize your situation sooner. Likewise, if you recognize it sooner, you get to the point where you can have one awful trade, just one (sort of like one potato chip or one chocolate chip cookie). Instead of turning into a gorge-fest, you have a psychological strategy to fall back on. Then you will have made it.

It is rarely, if ever, that first loser that kills you, it is almost *always* what comes after it.

In Chicago, they used to say, "Your first loss is your best loss," and it is true. Furthermore, if you manage to a strategy of psychological capital and leverage, oftentimes you will have your signal to take a break before you even get a chance for the second loss.

The BIKB—The "But I Know Better" Trade

The BIKB trade is that one you really regret. It is the one that you really didn't want to take but then again couldn't help yourself. It is the one that you get the maddest at yourself for. Why? Because you know better and you know you know better.

Nevertheless, even in a case where the meltdown isn't spectacular, the process is the same. First, let yourself feel bad. In fact, try actively to feel as badly as you can about making a mistake. Once again, a feeling can't in and of itself hurt you; it is just a feeling and once it gets your attention is likely to roll right on out of there. We are taught to not feel what we feel. We are taught to use our intellects to override how we feel. We are taught to reframe how we feel.

But I will tell you what, just feeling how you feel, and particularly feeling it for what it is and not some derivative, will save you a boatload of hassle and ultimately make you a lot more money. As the wife of a client once said, "Well, your head won't blow off."

In fact, if you don't go through this process, you can bet on a losing streak. I've seen it hundreds of times now—as well as the reverse, ending a losing streak by retracing one's steps to where the BIKB happened.

On the other hand, if you keep an eye out for all the variations of feelings you will have—anticipate them—then those feeling and emotional contexts don't automatically become the unknown canvas coloring your perception of the next trade. You have already examined it and you have already felt it. Your brain knows you got the message and is satisfied that your neurons, synapses, and glial cells are less likely to forget the next time.

Let Yourself Celebrate

In fact, force yourself to celebrate when things go brilliantly!

In this case, consciously act out that real feeling, that one where you get the next million dollar paycheck. Delve fully and completely into it. Why?

Want to know why winning streaks turn to losing streaks? The answer remains the same—people are acting out a context of feelings. They throw caution to the wind in the overconfidence that makes them think they have a golden touch.

Feeling the feeling, knowing what it is and why, and putting it into words short circuits that process. If you manage to your level of mental capital and psychological leverage first, you know when you feel "over the moon." You should also know, though, that this feeling carries the same risk signal as being tired or angry. It creates a context that skews your perception. It changes your beliefs, at least for the time being. If you revel instead, you can feel the feeling—really enjoy it—but keep it out of your account. All in all, that is a very good deal—deeply felt pleasure, extra clarity in uncertainty, and a high likelihood of another good decision.

Think of the multiplier! You get the first good trade, avoid the trading out of an overconfident emotional context, keep the money, and set yourself up to take the next trade with just the right amount of psychological capital. Now that is leverage!

Success Is a *Skill* and Not a Destination

In one way or another, I have coached about 2,000 traders since I founded The ReThink Group and TraderPsyches. Many of my clients have told me that improving their trading has turned out to be a journey of learning about themselves more than a journey of learning about the markets. Sure, they could put together a string of good trades but then something always happened, and they didn't understand why things fell apart, particularly at that moment. They had trouble getting things back together; sometimes it takes months or even years. Just like the day to day resembles being a quarterback, the long run resembles a marathon. I understand how you want to get to the end point and you will make leaps where you will look back and say, "Wow, this is much easier than I made it out to be"; but in trading, you always have to keep running. The markets have many personalities and what works with one doesn't work with the other. It can take a lifetime to get good at them all or give up on the ones that just don't suit your internal rhythm.

The thing you have to go on now is that our understanding of brain science just a few short years ago is analogous to when we thought the Earth was flat. Now that you indeed know that the Earth is round and that your brain is an emotional-context operator, you can sail across whatever waves the market throws your way. In doing so, your beliefs that Markowitz pointed out were so important and the perceptions and judgments that rely on those beliefs will be much more about the here and now and much less about what came before.

Chapter 22

Take It to the Next Level

Aeroport de Nice, Côte d'Azur, April 18, 2016

Neither Renee nor Michael could really believe it. As they waited for a taxi, Renee couldn't help but remember how a chance meeting in a taxi line in Chicago had landed them here, now, in Nice, France almost exactly five years later.

Tomorrow, they would pitch an investment in their fund to the chief investment officer and his staff of a family office based in Monaco! Almost a year ago, they had attended the biggest asset management conference in Europe and had been lucky enough to strike up a conversation during welcoming cocktails with a member of Monaco's government, who was in attendance as the country's official welcoming consul. With a startled flash in his eyes as they said, "Coup d'État Capital," he had asked them about the admittedly provocative name of their fund.

"Do you have a country in mind?" he had asked with a friendly laugh.

When they had explained that the coup was one of taking a psychological and qualitative approach to markets, which implicitly meant an overthrow of the dominance of numbers, he had congratulated them for their creativity and courage to buck the establishment and asked for them to consider presenting to their royal family's family office.

It had been almost a year, but now they were back. This would be their second pitch to a potential investor with serious money. Tom, Michael's brother, had come on board into a marketing role after his doctors had advised a year of physical therapy, which prevented him from fulfilling all his ski patrol duties, and he had almost immediately closed an investment through his Aspen contacts. They doubted they could get him to stay another year as Chicago was just too darn flat for either his skis or his bike; but so far he had done a great job with building their pitch book, making introductions, and even seeming to intuitively understand the markets. They joked that his name Tom truly did mean the same as it did in academic circles—"theory of mind"—their bedrock trading strategy.

And here they were almost ready to speak to those managing some of the wealth of one of the world's most prominent families. They had it planned to a "T." Renee would open with a brief layperson's introduction of the brain on risk and uncertainty—social and emotional context—and segue into how they used that foundation plus a risk management strategy built on psychological capital to look at both markets and money management in a unique way. Michael would then describe their work in detail.

And it had worked! Coup d'État would get a new investor, and a world class one at that.

*　*　*

Michael and Renee both silently wished they could stay in Monaco, but this trip didn't come cheaply and the fund was paying; neither had even broached the idea of a single vacation day. Now as they sat on the runway in Paris, having barely made their connection from Nice, the voice of the captain came ominously over the loudspeaker to announce a 45-minute delay.

Michael groaned and Renee rolled her eyes. Once they had gotten their heads around the fact that they must return as soon as possible, they were both impatient to get there. The founding members of the firm would be impressed. With Monaco, they would be going over $25 million of which they could claim more than 50% was due to Michael's comeback performance and subsequent capital raises.

Christopher for his part had admitted that forcing Michael out that day was one of the hardest things he had ever done. He knew no trader ever easily recovers from either a disaster or someone else stepping in to force them out of positions. But he also told them all how impressed he was with Michael's ultimate recovery from what they jokingly referred to as his attempt at a "coup de flop." Now no one in the firm forgot to anchor everything they did within a framework of mental capital and psychological leverage. They thought of themselves more like performers or athletes than financial types, and it was paying off.

Michael decided to stay put on the plane and sleep while Renee went back into the terminal to buy some gifts for the team. Unfortunately his sleep didn't last long. He no sooner got comfortable than the captain's voice boomed again with an announcement that the flight was now cancelled. On one hand it was exasperating; on the other hand, getting stuck overnight in Paris wasn't the same as getting stuck in, say, Dallas or Atlanta. He left the re-booking desk with their two hotel vouchers just as Renee showed back up at the gate.

"Well, guess what? We've got a free night in Paris! We're staying."

"Michael, stop it. We are not!" Renee said, as she absent-mindedly stuffed her receipts in the back of her passport folder.

"No, I'm not. They cancelled the whole flight. Here, look ..." he said, as he showed her their two hotel vouchers and confirmed boarding passes for a flight that left the next morning at 11.

"Wow, this is bizarre. But hey, what can we do? It's not our fault the plane isn't flying!" she said with a tiny giggle.

"If you ask me, this means we were supposed to celebrate!" said Michael.

Le Petit Retro Restaurant, April 19, 2016

Both Michael and Renee had been to Paris before and they knew two things, the Trocadéro neighborhood had plenty of good restaurants no matter which one they chose; and even dinner wine in France was better than anything by-the-glass in a good American restaurant. Under the circumstances, a little vino seemed more than appropriate, so they took the concierge's advice and walked the few minutes, in the surprisingly mild weather, to a highly rated local bistro.

Once they were seated, had had their toast to new capital and Renee had ordered for them in her in broken French, Michael took her by surprise with, "Ree, now that we have a free moment, can I talk to you about something that has been on my mind for quite a while?"

"Well, sure, I guess," she said while thinking, "why is he bringing up a problem now?" "What is it, Michael?"

Pushing back his chair, Michael stood up just far enough to clear the decanter. He gracefully bent over their tiny table and before she realized what he was doing, she felt his lips precisely meet hers—an emotional context that neither needed any consulting help to comprehend.

Afterword

You probably decided to read this book thinking it would be about how to beat the market, about how the market really works. And at this point, you might be thinking, that isn't at all what this book is about. You didn't expect that you would be reading about how you unconsciously fall into clusters of perception and expectations that began as experiences you had somewhere between conception and your teenage years, and most likely on the earlier rather than later half of that span. You thought you intended to learn how to better analyze the numerical dance of market numbers.

Here's the moral of the story: once you become familiar and hopefully facile with consciously contextualizing or curating market information in terms of who is or will be taking the other side of your trade, once you give up on finding "the (nonexistent) facts," the mind game of the markets *is* in your mind—and nowhere else. The perceptions belong to you, the interpretations are yours, and the one pushing the button, no matter what your timeframe, is either you or your ego.

Everything will fall prey to your ego and your unconscious, unless you make both conscious. You can leave the unconscious where it is, but that will be your biggest risk factor. Sooner or later it will burn you. "The Street," as it's known to those of us who professionally tend to the garden of Wall Street, is littered with examples, many of them repeats.

Think you are not susceptible to your own ego? Think there are guys out there who don't know a thing about how they really feel and yet are billionaires? There may be, although I would argue they know themselves better than their press agents ever let on. The other thing they certainly know is that markets are at their core only human games, not mathematical ones. They know this even if they spend all their time developing algorithms to stalk the cadence of the market's language. The numbers represent the playing cards and winning is way more about the mind games of playing poker, hands down, than anything else.

Regardless of whether every billion-dollar portfolio manager knows himself or herself or not, you can. And in doing so, you create an insurmountable edge that no changing market regime or market multiple personality disorder can take away from you. Spend half of your time working on yourself and you will make more progress than if you spent all of that time trying to figure out the next great unknown piece of information.

If you do, and I hope you will, then for every time you put your mental capital and psychological leverage first in your decision sequence, you can be guaranteed that at least for that trade, your outcome will be better than it would have been.

Imagine what will happen by the end of the year if you do that even just 50% more of the time than you do now?

Acknowledgments

Naturally, I have a long list of people to thank for their contribution to this book. In chronological order, I must first thank Joan Rich, PhD of Cleveland, Ohio, for first introducing me in 1986 to the fact that I could misinterpret someone in adult life as acting just like (and making me feel just like) my father did.

Next, I would like to extend my thanks to the University of Chicago and their foresight to offer a master's program where you can research just about anything you want. Martha McClintock agreed to advise me on a thesis in what has become neuropsychoanalysis long before there was an official field known as such.

Alas, however, Don Winton, who had been ZAP on the trading floors, came along and diverted me from a PhD into trading. Not only for doing so, but for his many lessons in tape reading, as well as life, he will always have my deepest gratitude.

Gail Osten, now of the Chicago Board Options Exchange, published my first article in 2004. Putting "Freud's Path to Profits" in a magazine called *Stocks, Futures and Options* had to take some guts. It also altered my trajectory in ways I could have never imagined.

Deborah Greene Bershatsky extended what I knew about psychoanalytic thinking and provided enormous support for the idea of a "talking traders" group and this book. To Gene, Marika, Jeff, and Tracy, thanks for hanging in there while I have been figuring out all of this.

Of course, then come my many clients who have shared their struggles and their triumphs—Mike, Scott, Robert, Jenny from "Down Under," and

Dave—the list runs long but for each of you (a book-length list) who have contributed to my thinking and who have thanked me for helping you, I am deeply grateful.

To Jennifer, Joe, Lydia, and Sara at McGraw-Hill, I can only say thank you for putting up with me. It isn't easy to work with someone as passionate about their work as I am. Thank you for giving me the chance and for trying to make this book the best it can be. All errors are of course mine and mine alone.

To Clay, thanks for the research work and to Chrissy Sidler and Abby Ranson, I promise, next time I will ask for the bibliographic corrections earlier in the process!

Last, to William T. Long III, merci beaucoup beaucoup (yep, that is two) for generously sharing your copious knowledge, not only in economics but in so many other fields. You never will know how much I have learned from you.

Bibliography

Prologue

"The Audit." *Columbia Journalism Review*. http://www.cjr.org/the_audit/covering_the_republicans_crisi.php.

Shull, Denise. "The Neurobiology of Freud's Repetition Compulsion." *Annals of Modern Psychoanalysis*. 2003, 2(1): 21–46.

Taleb, Nassim. *The Black Swan: The Impact of the Highly Improbable*. New York: Random House, 2007.

Chapter 2

Ambady, Nalini. "The Mind in the World: Culture and the Brain." http://www.psychologicalscience.org/index.php/publications/observer/2011/may-june–11/page/2.

The Wall Street Journal. "Lost in Translation." July 24, 2010.

Bernstein, P. *Against the Gods: The Remarkable Story of Risk*. New York: Wiley, 1996.

Patterson, S. *The Quants: How a New Breed of Math Whizzes Conquered Wall Street and Nearly Destroyed It*. New York: Crown Business, 2010.

Cioffi, R. and Tannin, M. "Verdict: Ex-Bear Stearns Hedge Fund Managers NOT GUILTY on ALL Fraud Charges." *Huffpost Business*. November 10, 2009. http://www.huffingtonpost.com.

Mandelbrot, Benoit B. *Fractals and Scaling in Finance: Discontinuity, Concentration, Risk. Selecta Volume E*. New York: Springer, 1997.

Mandelbrot, Benoit B. *The (Mis)Behavior of Markets: A Fractal View of Risk, Ruin and Reward*. New York: Basic Books, 2004.

Schmeidler, David. "Subjective Probability and Expected Utility without Additivity." *Econometrica* 57, no. 3 (1989): 571–587. http://www.jstor.org/pss/1911053.

Epstein, Larry. "A Definition of Uncertainty Aversion." *The Review of Economic Studies* 66, no. 3 (1999): 579–608. http://onlinelibrary.wiley.com/.

Ellsberg, Daniel. "Risk, Ambiguity, and the Savage Axioms." *Quarterly Journal of Economics* 75, no. 4 (1961): 643–669. doi:10.2307/1884324.

Hotz, Robert Lee. "Atlas Gives Scientists New View of the Brain." *The Wall Street Journal*, April 13, 2011.

Fields, R. Douglas. *The Other Brain*. New York: Simon & Schuster, 2010.

Ferrucci, David. "Man Made Minds: Living with Thinking Machines." Panel, World Science Festival, Hunter College; New York, June 4, 2011.

Chapter 3

Knight, Frank H. *Risk, Uncertainty, and Profit, 1st edition*. Houghton Mifflin Company, 1921.

Markowitz, H. M. "Portfolio Selection." *The Journal of Finance* 7, no. 1 (March 1952): 77–91. doi:10.2307/2975974. JSTOR†2975974.

Abodeely, J. J. "Modern Portfolio Theory Is Harming Your Portfolio." *Pragmatic Capitalism*, June 7, 2011. http://pragcap.com/modern-portfolio-theory-is-harming-your-portfolio.http://pragcap.com/modern-portfolio-theory-is-harming-your-portfolio.

Patterson, Scott. *The Quants. How a New Breed of Math Whizzes Conquered Wall Street and Nearly Destroyed It.* United States: Crown Business, 2010.

The Wall Street Journal. "Letting the Machines Decide." July 14, 2010.

Chapter 4

Hunt, Morton. *The Story of Psychology.* New York: Anchor Books, 1993, 2007.

Freud, Sigmund. "Project for Scientific Psychology." *The Standard Edition of the Complete Psychological Works of Sigmund Freud,* 1 (1953): 283–397.

Ferguson, Niall. *The Ascent of Money: a Financial History of the World.* New York: Penguin Press, 2008.

Darwin, Charles. *The expression of emotion in man and animals.* Champaign Il: Project Gutenberg, 199. Print.

Mesquita, Batja, Barrett, Lisa Feldman, and Smith, Eliot R. *The Mind in Context.* New York: The Guilford Press, 2010.

Fields, R. Douglas. *The Other Brain.* New York: Simon & Schuster, 2010.

Damasio, Antonio R. *Descartes' Error: Emotion, Reason, and the Human Brain.* New York: Putnam, 1994.

Barrett, Lisa Feldman and Bar, Moshe. "See It with Feeling: Affective Predictions during Object Perception." *Philosophical Transactions of The Royal Society* 364 (2009): 1325–1334.

Camerer, Colin, Loewenstein, George, and Prelec, Drazen. "Neuroeconomics: How Neuroscience Can Inform Economics." *The Journal of Economic Literature* 43 (2005): 9–64.

Seo, Myeong-Gu and Barrett, Lisa Feldman, "Being Emotional During Decision Making –Good or Bad? An Empirical Investigation." *PubMed Central* 50, no. 4 (2007): 923–940.

"Never let emotions cloud your judgment" textbook financial advice HSBC. "HSBC Premier." Advertisement. *The Financial Times* (London). 2010

Ferrucci, David. "Man Made Minds: Living with Thinking Machines." Lecture, World Science Festival, Hunter College; New York, June 4, 2011.

Browning, E. S. and Strausburg, Jenny. "The Mutual Fund in the 'Flash Crash'." *The Wall Street Journal*, October 7, 2010.

McTague, Jim. "The Real Flash-Crash Culprits." *The Wall Street Journal*, October 11, 2010.

Inauguration of President Franklin Delano Roosevelt, 1933. Joint Congressional Committee on Inaugural Ceremonies. http://inaugural.senate.gov/history/chronology/fdroosevelt1933.cfm.

Chapter 5

Pastore, S., Ponta, L., and Cincotti, S. *Stock Market Model First to Reproduce Main Properties of Real Market.* Issue brief no. 198325309. July 14, 2010. www.physorg.com. From Heterogeneous information-based artificial stock market. S. Pastore, L. Ponta and S. Cincotti, *New Journal of Physics* (2010): 053035.

Chapter 6

Keynes, John Maynard. *The General Theory of Employment, Interest and Money.* New York: Harcourt, Brace and Company, 1935.

Battle of the Quants Conference. Marriott Marquis, New York, February 16, 2011.

Investment Decisions and Behavioral Finance. Harvard Kennedy School, November 5–6, 2009.

Landman, Janet. *Regret: the Persistence of the Possible*. New York: Oxford University Press, 1993.

Shull, Denise. "Probability vs. Ambiguity" *CME Magazine*, Spring 2009. http://www.cmegroup.com.

Van Overwalle, Frank, and Baetens, Kris. "Understanding Others' Actions and Goals by Mirror and Mentalizing Systems: A Meta-analysis." *NeuroImage* 48, no. 3 (2009): 564–84. doi:10.1016/j.neuroimage.2009.06.009.

Bruguier, A. J., Quartz, S. B., and Bossaerts, P. "Exploring the Nature of 'Trader Intuition'." *The Journal of Finance*, 65, no. 5 (2010): 1703–1723.

Cosmides, L., and Tooby, J. Cognitive adaptations for social exchange. In J. Barkow, L. Cosmides, and J. Tooby (eds.), *The Adapted Mind*. New York: Oxford University Press, 1992.

Burrough, Bryan. "Wall Street's Most Secretive Mogul Speaks." *Vanity Fair*, July 2010.

Taub, Stephen. "The Rich List." *Absolute Return*, April 2011.

Hedgeworld News. "US Senator Grassley Steps Up Pressure on SEC in SAC Probe." June 16, 2011.

LeFerve, Edwin. *Reminiscence of a Stock Operator, A Market Place Book*. Hoboken, NJ: Wiley, 1994.

Lo, Andrew W. "The Adaptive Markets Hypothesis." *The Journal of Portfolio Management* 30, no. 5 (2004): 15–29. doi:10.3905/jpm.2004.442611.

Brooks, David. *The Social Animal: the Hidden Sources of Love, Character, and Achievement*. New York: Random House, 2011.

Ross Sorkin, Andrew. *Too Big To Fail*. New York: Penguin, 2010.

The Wall Street Journal. "The Mutual Fund in the Flash Crash," October 2, 2010.

Chapter 7

Ambady, Nalini. "The Mind in the World: Culture and the Brain." http://www.psychologicalscience.org/index.php/publications/observer/2011/may-june–11/page/2.

Mesquita, Batja, Barrett, Lisa Feldman, and Smith, Eliot R. *The Mind in Context*. New York: Guilford Press, 2010.

Mesquita, Batja. "Emotions as dynamic cultural phenomena." In R. J. Davidson, K. R. Scherer, and H. H. Goldsmith (eds), *Handbook of Affective Sciences*. New York: Oxford University Press, 2003: 871–890.

Frege, Gottlob. *The Foundations of Arithmetic*. Trans. J. L. Austin. Second revised ed. Evanston, IL: Northwestern University Press, 1980.

Hsu, M., Bhatt, M., Adolphs, R., Tranel, D., and Cramerer, F. "Neutral Systems Responding to Degrees of Uncertainty in Human Decision-Making." *Science* 310 (2005).

Platt, Michael L. and Huettel, Scott A. "Risky Business: The Neuroeconomics of Decision Making under Uncertainty." *Nature Neuroscience* 11, no. 4 (2008): 398–403. doi:10.1038/nn2062.

Chapter 8

The Wall Street Journal. "Unprecedented String of 400 Point Swings." August 13, 2011.

CNBC. "Markets in Turmoil Special Report." August 12, 2011.

Kuhnen, C. M. and Knutson, B. "The Influence of Affect on Beliefs, Preferences and Financial Decisions." *Journal of Finance and Quantitative Analysis* 46, no. 3 (2011): 605–626.

Kuhnen, C. M. and Knutson, B. "The Neural Basis of Financial Risk Taking" *Neuron* 47, no. 5 (2005): 763–770.

Barrett, L. F. and Bar, M. "See It with Feeling: Affective Predictions during Object Perception." *Philosophical Transactions of the Royal Society B: Biological Sciences* 364, no. 1521 (2009): 1325–334. doi:10.1098/rstb.2008.0312.

Elliot, A. J. and Aarts, H. "Perception of the Colour Red Enhances the Force and Velocity of Motor Output." *Emotion*, 11, no. 2 (2011): 445–449.

Chapter 9

Akerlof, George A. and Robert J. Shiller. *Animal Spirits: How Human Psychology Drives the Economy, and Why It Matters for Global Capitalism.* Princeton, NJ: Princeton University Press, 2009.

Sammon, Paul. *Future Noir: The Making of Blade Runner.* New York: HarperPrism, 1996.

Barad, J. and Robertson, E. *The Ethics of Start Trek.* New York: Harper-Collins, 2000.

Damasio, Antonio. *The Feeling of What Happens. Body and Emotion in the Marketing of Consciousness.* London: Vintage, 2000.

Darwin, Charles. *The expression of emotion in man and animals.* Champaign Il: Project Gutenberg, 199. Print.

Ross Sorkin, Andrew. *Too Big To Fail.* New York: Penguin, 2010.

The Wall Street Journal. "Clashing Testimony Over Lehman," September 2, 2010.

Chapter 10

Steidlmayer, J. Peter and Steidlmayer, Heidy. *New Market Discoveries.* Kirbmarn, 1990.

Chapter 11

Venkatraman, V., Huettal, S., Chuah, L., Payne, J., and Chee, M. "Sleep Deprivation Biases the Neural Mechanisms Underlying Economic Preferences." *The Journal of Neuroscience*, 31, no. 10 (2011): 3712–3718.

Venkatraman, Vinod." Strategic Variability in Risky Choice: Mechanisms and Implications for Neuroanatomy of Cognitive Control." Dissertation, Department of Psychology and Neuroscience, Duke University, 2011.

Urrila, A. S., Hakkarainen, A., Heikkinen, S., et al. "Metabolic Imaging of Human Cognition: An fMRI Study of Brain Lactate Response to Silent Word Generation." *Journal of Cerebral Blood Flow and Metabolism*, 23 (2003): 942–948.

Ross Sorkin, Andrew. *Too Big To Fail*. New York: Penguin, 2010.

Alberini, Christina. "Dynamic Memory Traces." Lecture, Arnold Pfeffer Center for Neuropsychoanalysis, New York Psychoanalytic Institute, New York Psychoanalytic Society, New York, June 4, 2011.

Chapter 12

Gladwell, Malcolm. *blink: the Power of Thinking without Thinking*. New York: Little, Brown and Company, 2005.

Kahneman, Daniel and Tversky, Amos. "Prospect Theory an Analysis of Decision under Risk." *Econometrica* XLVII (1979): 263–91.

LeDoux, Joseph, Damasio, Antonio, and Kandel, Eric. "The Anxious Brain." *Charlie Rose Brain Series*. PBS. May 26, 2010. http://www.charlierose.com/view/collection/10702.

Brooks, David. *The Social Animal: the Hidden Sources of Love, Character, and Achievement*. New York: Random House, 2011.

Fields, R. Douglas. *The Other Brain*. New York: Simon & Schuster, 2010.

Fields, Douglas. "Mysterious Cells Found in Einstein's Brain." *Odyssey*, November 1, 2009.

Mesquita, Batja, Barrett, Lisa Feldman, and Smith, Eliot R. *The Mind in Context*. New York: Guilford Press, 2010.

Eagleman, David. *Incognito, The Hidden Life of the Brain*. New York: Random Pantheon Books, 2011.

Insel, Thomas R. "Toward a Neurobiology of Attachment." *Review of General Psychology* 4, no. 2 (2000): 176–85.

Schore, Allan. "The Effects of a Secure Attachment Relationship on Right Brain Development, Affect Regulation and Infant Mental Health." *Infant Mental Health Journal*, 2001, 7–66. http://www.trauma-pages.com/articles.php#Schore.

Alberini, Christina. "Dynamic Memory Traces." Lecture, Arnold Pfeffer Center for Neuropsychoanalysis, New York Psychoanalytic Institute, New York Psychoanalytic Society, New York, June 4, 2011.

Gross, J. J. and Barrett, L. F. "Emotion Generation and Emotion Regulation: One or Two Depends on Your Point of View." *Emotion Review*. 3 (2011): 8–16.

Barrett, L. F. and Bar, M. "See It with Feeling: Affective Predictions during Object Perception." *Philosophical Transactions of the Royal Society B: Biological Sciences* 364, no. 1521 (2009): 1325–334. doi:10.1098/rstb.2008.0312.

Camerer, Colin, Loewenstein, George, and Prelec, Drazen. "Neuroeconomics: How Neuroscience Can Inform Economics." *Journal of Economic Literature* XLIII (March 2005): 9–64.

Vytal, Katherine and Hamann, Stephan. "Neuroimaging Support for Discrete Neural Correlates of Basic Emotions: A Voxel-based Meta-analysis." *Journal of Cognitive Neuroscience* 22, no. 12 (2010): 2864–885. doi:10.1162/jocn.2009.21366.

Barrett, Lisa Feldman and Wager, Tor D. "The Structure of Emotion. Evidence From Neuroimaging Studies." *Current Directions in Psychological Science* 15, no. 2 (2006): 79–83. doi:10.1111/j.0963-7214.2006.00411.

Lerner, Jennifer S. and Keltner, Dacher. "Fear, Anger, and Risk." *Journal of Personality and Social Psychology* 81, no. 1 (2001): 146–59. doi: 10.1037//0022-3514.81.1.146.

Lerner, J. S. and Tiedens, L. Z. "Portrait of the Angry Decision Maker: How Appraisal Tendencies Shape Anger's Influence on Cognition." *Journal of Behavioral Decision Making,* 19 (2006): 115–137.

Keltner, Dacher and Lerner, Jennifer. "Emotion." In Susan Fiske and Daniel Gilbert (eds.), *Handbook of Social Psychology*, 5th ed., vol. 1. New York: Wiley, 2010.

Cozolino, Louis J. *The Neuroscience of Psychotherapy: Building and Rebuilding the Human Brain.* New York: Norton, 2002.

Nahl, Diane and Bilal, Dania (eds.). *Information and Emotion: The Emergent Affective Paradigm in Information Behavior Research and Theory.* Medford, NJ: American Society for Information Science and Technology, 2007.

Chapter 13

Schur, Ted. "Ted on Ambiguity." *Psychological Capital* [blog]. December 17, 2010. www.traderpsyches.com.

Ferguson, Niall. *The Ascent of Money: a Financial History of the World.* New York: Penguin, 2008.

"His Brain: Her Brain, How We Are Different." *Scientific American Mind,* May/June 2010.

Tannen, Deborah. *You Just Don't Understand: Women and Men in Conversation.* New York: Quill, 2001.

Sommer, Jeff. "How Men's Overconfidence Hurts Them as Investors." *The New York Times*, March 14, 2010.

Landman, Janet. *Regret: the Persistence of the Possible*. New York: Oxford University Press, 1993.

Bell, D. E. "Regret in Decision Making under Uncertainty." *Operations Research* 30, no. 5 (1982): 961–81. doi:10.1287/opre.30.5.961.

Loomes, G. and R. Sugden. "Regret Theory: An Alternative Theory of Rational Choice under Uncertainty." *The Economic Journal* 92 (1982): 805–924.

Sugden, Robert. "Regret, Recrimination and Rationality." *Theory and Decision* 19, no. 1 (1985): 77–99. doi:10.1007/BF00134355.

Chapter 14

Mandelbrot, Benoit B. *The (Mis)Behavior of Markets: A Fractal View of Risk, Ruin and Reward*. New York: Basic Books, 2004.

Mandelbrot, Benoit B. *Fractals and Scaling in Finance: Discontinuity, Concentration, Risk : Selecta Volume E*. New York: Springer, 1997.

Marshall, Robert. "Mirroring and Fractals: Integrating Concepts in Psychoanalysis." Draft copy provided prior to Marshall 2010 lecture, Center for Modern Psychoanalysis, New York.

Wyer, Robert S. and Bargh, John A. *The Automaticity of Everyday Life*. Mahwah, NJ: Lawrence Erlbaum Associates, 1997.

Brooks, David. *The Social Animal: the Hidden Sources of Love, Character, and Achievement*. New York: Random House, 2011.

Eagleman, David. *Incognito, The Hidden Life of the Brain*. New York: Random Pantheon Books, 2011.

Freud, Sigmund and Strachey, James. *Introductory Lectures on Psychoanalysis*. New York: Norton, 1977.

Alberini, Christina. "Dynamic Memory Traces." Lecture, Arnold Pfeffer Center for Neuropsychoanalysis, New York Psychoanalytic Institute, New York Psychoanalytic Society, New York, June 4, 2011.

Freud, Sigmund and Strachey, James. *Beyond the Pleasure Principle.* New York: Norton, 1989.

LaPlanche, Jean and Pontalis, J. B. *The Language of Psychoanalysis.* New York: Norton, 1974.

Tamietto, Marco and De Gelder, Beatrice. "Neural Bases of the Non-conscious Perception of Emotional Signals." *Nature Reviews Neuroscience* 11, no. 10 (2010): 697–709. doi:10.1038/nrn2889.

Mesulam, M. "From Sensation to Cognition." *Brain* 121 (1998):10131–10152.

Treue, S. "Climbing the Cortical Ladder from Sensation to Perception." *Trends in Cognitive Sciences* 7, no. 11 (2003): 469–71. doi:10.1016/j.tics.2003.09.003.

Fonagy, Peter. "Attachment Theory and Psychoanalysis." *Journal of Child Psychotherapy*, 29 (2003): 109–115.

Fishman, Steve. "Madoff on Madoff, The Jailhouse Tapes." *New York*, March 7, 2011.

Shull, Denise. "Psychological Dynamics in a Madoff Made-Up World." *Hedgeworld* [blog], December 17, 2008.

Murphy, Megan. "Cash on Account but No Certain Location for the Rest." *The Financial Times* (London), March 2011.

Shull, Denise. "Would Raj Risk It All." *Absolute Return* [blog], April 2011. http://www.absolutereturn-alpha.com/AR-Magazine.

Chapter 16

Venkatraman, V., Huettal, S., Chuah, L., Payne, J., and Chee, M. "Sleep Deprivation Biases the Neural Mechanisms Underlying Economic Preferences." *The Journal of Neuroscience*, 31, no. 10 (2011): 3712– 3718.

McRae, Kateri, Supriya, Misra, Prasad, Aditya, Pereira, Sean, and Gross, James. (in press). "Bottom-up and Top-down Emotion Generation: Implications for Emotion Regulation." *Social Cognitive and Affective Neuroscience*.

Chapter 17

Hendrix, Harville. *Getting the Love You Want: A Guide for Couples*. New York: Henry Holt, 2008.

Margolis, Benjamin. "Mirroring, Psychological Reflection: Terminology, Definitions, Theoretical Considerations." *Modern Psychoanalysis*, XI, 1 & 2, 1986.

Vaughan, Susan C. *The Talking Cure: The Science behind Psychotherapy*. New York: Henry Holt, 1997.

LeDoux, Joseph E. *The Emotional Brain: the Mysterious Underpinnings of Emotional Life*. New York: Simon & Schuster, 1998.

Chapter 18

Linkoping University. "Intuition Can Be Explained." *ScienceDaily*, July 2, 2008.

Carey, Benedict. "In Battle, Hunches Prove to Be Valuable." *The New York Times*, July 28, 2008.

Dijksterhuis, Ap, Bos, Maarten W., Nordgren, Loran F., and van Baaren, Rick B. "On Making the Right Choice: The Deliberation-Without-Attention Effect."

Science (February 17, 2006): 311 (5763), 1005–1007. doi:10.1126/science. 1121629.

Smith, Lauren. "Helping Clients Find Their Feelings." Interview by author. November 28, 2010.

Treynor, Wendy, Gonzalez, Richard, and Nolen-Hoeksema, Susan. "Rumination Reconsidered: A Psychometric Analysis." *Cognitive Therapy and Research* (2003): 247–259.

Guerrero, Laura and Reiter, Renee. "Expressing Emotion: Sex Differences in Social Skills and Communicative Responses to Anger, Sadness and Jealousy." In *Sex Differences and Similarities in Communication: Critical Essays and Empirical Investigation of Sex and Gender in Interaction*. New York: Psychology Press, 1998: Chapter 14.

Index

A

AAPL, 57, 79, 83
Academia, Wall Street and, 3–7
Actions, emotions and, 94, 96, 224–225
Adaptive markets hypothesis, 67
Advanced workshop lectures
  fractal geometry playing market mind, 147–167
  mark-to-market emotions, 121–134
  mental capital and psychological leverage, 111–120
  regret theory, greed and, 135–145
Against the Gods (Bernstein), 12
AIG, 68–69, 114
Alcmaeon, 34
Allen, Paul, 17
alpha, 112, 120, 132
Ambient building blocks, 82–83
Ambient reality, 73–80
Ambiguity aversion, 14
Angelides, Phil, 96
Anger
  frustration turning into, 128–129, 132

turning into meltdown, 128–129
  as one of five basic emotions, 126
  role of, 37
Anthropomorphizing, 66–67
Anticipation
  of feelings, 228
  of regret, 142–144
Anxiety
  on FAD spectrum, 127–128
  of uncertainty, 136–138, 180
Apple, 57, 83. *See also* AAPL
Approach, 127
Aristotle, 34
Arithmetic, 73–74, 80
Army, intuition and, 198–199
The Ascent of Money (Ferguson), 139
asset allocation, Markowitz's concept of, 27–28
Athletes, market, 115–117
Attentive deliberation, 200
Auctions, 69–71
August 2007 market swings, probability of, 12
Automaticity, 127, 135
Avoidance, 127

M

proprietary, 3–4, 103–104
recovery in, 223–226
tiring, 114–115
traditional education, 11
Traditional trading education, 11
Training manual, Coup d'État
Capital, 223
Transference, 151, 163–164
Treasuries, US, 212
Trends, fighting, 160
Triune model, of brain, 37, 74,
122
Truth
existence of, 58
of speculation, 56–59
Twitter, scraping of, 105
2008 crash, 25, 29, 98

U

Uncertainty
anxiety of, 136–138, 180
circuit, 77–78
context of, 76–80
economics of, 28
lecture on dealing with,
53–72
neuroemotion and, 39–41
new psychology of, 112–113,
147–148
pain of, 195
poker illustrating, 24–25
reality and, 74–80
risk *v.*, 23
wagering and, 24–25
Unconscious brain
*f*C in, 159–163

F-eC in, 185–193
fractals and, 150–153, 159–163
pattern recognition and,
197–203
risk of, 235
Understanding, of other humans,
62–64
United States (US)
downgraded long-term debt of,
82
Treasuries, 212
Unmeasurability, reality of, 23
US. *See* United States

V

Value
assessment, 70
expected, 58
of experience, 106–108
fundamental, 55
Vanity Fair, 65
Vision, context of, 87–89
Volume, at price over time, 107
Vulcans, 93

W

Wager, Tor, 127
Wagering, uncertainty and,
24–25
Wall Street
academia and, 3–7
"Michael Kelley" on, 4–5, 45–53,
55, 68, 78, 97, 103
Water-skiing example, of beliefs,
46–48